The
Angry
Child

The Angry Child

Regaining Control When Your Child Is Out of Control

TIM MURPHY, PH.D.
and Loriann Hoff Oberlin

CLARKSON POTTER/PUBLISHERS
NEW YORK

Copyright © 2001 by Dr. Tim Murphy

Published by Clarkson Potter/Publishers, New York, New York. Member of the Crown Publishing Group.

Random House, Inc. New York, Toronto, London, Sydney, Auckland
www.randomhouse.com

Clarkson N. Potter is a trademark and Potter and colophon are registered trademarks of Random House, Inc.

Printed in the United States of America

Design by Maggie Hinders

Library of Congress Cataloging-in-Publication Data
Murphy, Timothy F.
        The angry child : regaining control when your child is out of control /
    by Timothy F. Murphy & Loriann Hoff Oberlin
            p. cm.
        Includes Index.
        1. Child psychology. 2. Anger in children. 3. Child rearing.
    I. Hoff Oberlin, Loriann, 1961– II. Title
    HQ 772 .M87 2001
    649'.64 dc21   2001016352

ISBN 0-609-60676-X

10 9 8 7 6 5 4 3 2 1

First Edition

All the anecdotes in the book are based on real-life experiences. They are adapted from stories told to me by parents and children in my psychological practice, from lectures and workshops, or through my radio and television appearances. However, all of the names used in this text are fictitious in order to protect the confidentiality essential for all clients. Identifying information and geographic location have been changed, and stories have been altered where necessary to protect the individuals and families involved. In some instances, composites of two or three persons have been used to obscure them and to clarify the relevant issues. Any similarities between the anecdotes presented and any actual person, living or deceased, is entirely coincidental.

a few. Working on talk shows, TV news segments, and special programs with Patrice King Brown, Jan Getz, Drew Moniot, Bruce Kaplan, Mary Flynn, and Paul Kelvyn of KDKA-TV taught me the ropes and gave me an opportunity to reach many families around the country. Phil Musick of WTAE Radio was not only a talk-show host, but he shared his microphone weekly with me for years, inviting callers to dial in and relying upon my insight. As an author himself, Phil encouraged me to put my ideas into print. Television producer Lynne Squilla continues to ask me probing questions about children, and this inspires me to learn more. I'm pleased to have played a part in some of her award-winning productions. And I thank WTAE-TV for including me in their "Success By Six" segments.

I can't forget about Michael Fields, formerly of WQED-TV, who encouraged me to pursue my political and psychology goals. And speaking of politics, I owe a great debt of thanks to Bob Jubelirer, the President Pro Tempore of the Pennsylvania Senate. It's a pleasure and inspiration to work side by side with someone who is so passionate about family issues, and who now encourages me to translate that scientific knowledge into laws and public policy. Judge Max Baer with the Allegheny County courts gave me much guidance on issues involving child custody and divorce.

The final stage of this project involved getting it into print. Piles of notes from lectures, professional journals, parenting articles; from encounters with families in my psychology practice; and from speaking engagements were compiled into outlines. This meant late nights at the computer keyboard long after my wife and daughter were asleep. Many portions of this manuscript were written just before I decided to run for the state senate.

The project then sat in a box until my coauthor, Loriann Hoff Oberlin, took an interest in it. With my senate duties demanding so much of my time, the manuscript would have remained in that box were it not for her diligence in updating it and crafting it into this finished product. I am very grateful to her for recognizing it was time to bring this book to the shelf and for seeing it through to completion. A special thanks to Jeff Herman for shepherding our proposal to a publisher, and to Pam Krauss at Crown Publishing/Random House for her skillful editing and guidance.

But through all of these stages runs a river of determination and confidence taught to me by my own parents. They had it rough, raising eleven children on a meager income. As a family, we certainly had our share of fights, laughter, disappointments, and joy over the years. But the devotion of my parents to their children, and their faith in God, continues to inspire me to help others overcome obstacles in their lives.

—Dr. Tim Murphy

Contents

Part 2 Strategies for Coping with and Preventing Anger

Introduction

I T'S HARD to pinpoint the exact moment the change occurs. One day your otherwise sunny child is merely prone to the occasional nasty outburst, and the next a permanent storm cloud seems to have taken up residence over her head. Small social problems or household disagreements escalate into major battles that leave all participants wounded and wary. Your once predictable child has become more than temperamental; you never know when the next meltdown will occur—or where. And the effort of trying to control these outbursts—or avoid them at any cost—may be impacting on how you deal with others in your family, social circle, and your child's school.

If you have a child whose anger and rage holds your family emotionally hostage, embarrasses you in public, or intimidates you and others with threats of violence or vicious comments, you know exactly what I'm talking about. It may come in the form of a toddler's tantrums or a teenager's tirade, in silent refusals or violent rage. Whichever form it takes, this anger is destroying our children and our families, and it's becoming epidemic.

You probably know how difficult it is to convince friends and family that your four- or fourteen-year-old is terrorizing your house. But it's true. Anger, especially out-of-control anger, is without a doubt one of the most demanding situations parents regularly face. Most children have occasional outbursts, but sooner rather than later they calm down and life goes on. A single outburst does not make an "angry child." Unchecked, however, continued anger is a sign that something is terribly wrong and must be addressed—soon.

Does this mean that today's difficult four-year-old will turn into tomorrow's headline maker? Not at all. But parents need to know that unless the tide of anger is turned, an angry child will grow into the angry adult who perpetuates an unhealthy cycle of active abuse or passive aggression. It's never too early to start helping your child bring his or her anger under control. Adopting the strategies that follow will aid you in doing exactly that.

This book grew out of my work as a child psychologist. For more than twenty years I've helped children understand their anger, working with both them and their families. During that time, I've seen that amazing turnarounds are possible. In this book I'll tell it as I've come to understand it, for while you might know an angry child or two, I've worked with hundreds of them. The good news is that most of them are delightful kids with bright futures. But they are at a crossroads, and often there's great urgency to helping them travel the correct path before they've gone too far astray.

As I reached for books to recommend for my patients, I found there were none I felt comfortable with. Some of the guidance was outdated. Some was skewed toward only the most violent children. Some was too research-oriented and lacked practical advice. Many books and mental health professionals still advocated old anger management methods, such as yelling or punching a pillow, while visualizing the image of the person with whom one might be upset. But as a parent, would you allow your son or daughter to play with matches and gasoline to satisfy a curiosity about fire? Why, then, would you allow your child to stage angry outbursts to let off steam?

The child who vents her anger by using bad language around the house, smashing toys, or unleashing her anger on others feels the false sense that "since I feel better when I let out my anger, this must be the right thing to do." She mistakes the feeling of relief for resolution. These are misguided methods of handling anger. They reinforce the idea that lashing out, disrespecting others while losing one's temper, are okay if you're angry. But it's never okay to lash out or attack when angry. Although it's sometimes okay to be angry, it's never okay to be mean. When you reinforce the connection between anger and a violent outburst, the child will surely attack aggressively the next time.

In 1999, Dr. Brad J. Bushman, an associate professor of psychology at Iowa State University, led a study on letting out aggression.[1] He and his colleagues described venting as poor practice. In layman's terms, this study's subjects who were given the message that hitting objects was an effective way of venting anger and then actually hit a punching bag were later more aggressive toward their rivals. It's a matter of displaced aggression, sometimes directed toward an innocent third party.

Venting, therefore, is not the solution I want to give parents, teachers, other therapists, and anyone else with a vested interest in teaching children that anger need not be a way of life. What they need are easy-to-follow strategies for coping with all the conflicts, both large and small, that arise each day. I'll show you how to fight fair when arguments arise, and how to administer discipline in such a way that a child's self-esteem remains intact. You'll find helpful methods for conquering the angry child's resistance to everyday chores and responsibilities without incurring their resentment, and ideas for ameliorating the effects of divorce on those caught in the cross fire. These strategies, together with a caring, involved parent, can douse the embers of a child's anger and eliminate the constant fear that the fire will rekindle at any moment.

I wrote this book to give parents and others a more comprehensive yet practical approach to handling anger. As you read it, you should get a better understanding of your child and your role in helping him or her cope with angry impulses. If you need to seek help beyond this book, your child's doctor may be your first stop for professional support. This book will help you formulate questions to ask yourself and the doctor: Has this reached the level where I need help? Is this more than just a prolonged bad mood? What can I do to help him change? Is there hope?

But true change takes work. It requires, first, understanding the genesis of an individual child's reservoir of anger and the specific ways in which it manifests itself. There is no single strategy that is right for every child and every family. (Since anger knows no gender boundaries, I'll try to interchange pronouns to reflect both boys and girls. Truly, the characteristics can apply to both.)

For some parents, working toward calming their child's anger will require a close examination of their own relationship with anger. I wish I could sugarcoat much of this material, but I cannot. From my perspective, I liken it to going to a medical doctor time and again with certain symptoms. If you finally found out there was something you were doing to cause or worsen your ailments, I'm sure you'd be frustrated that the doctor didn't share this with you at the first visit. I firmly believe most parents want only the best for their children, and they'd go to almost any lengths to ensure a happy future for them—even if it means altering their own behavior.

In my role as a member of the Pennsylvania State Senate, I've faced a broad range of social concerns affecting children and adults, not only in my home district but nationwide. There is a constant public outcry for a legislative fix for society's problems. Although I believe there may be times government can help, I feel even more strongly that the real solutions lie in strong families. The solutions do not come from the state house. Rather, they must come from everyone's house. Instead of making laws that affect children after they commit a crime, I'd like to see us solve some of these issues at the root level so that no child, no family, no community, must deal with the aftermath of rage.

When society fails to stop anger at its source, violence ensues. With this book, I hope those who care about children's anger will embrace new strategies. It takes practice, hard work, persistence, and, yes, time. Be patient. There is much hope. And if you struggle with persistent anger in your child, in yourself, or in your family, seek the help of a trained psychotherapist. This book may offer you tremendous insight, but it's in no way meant to replace the intervention of a professional.

In *The Angry Child*, I don't claim to have every answer. I can't even claim to be the perfect parent myself. Who can? I do think, however, that together we can harness the hysteria of news headlines and take some real ownership of anger in our world. The challenge of halting childhood anger may seem daunting, but if we get to the root of the problem, we can make important headway toward resolution.

part 1

Understanding Anger

all been there after a hard day, left wondering if negotiating world peace would be a simpler task than getting our children to clear the table or finish their homework. And much of the time we're simply baffled by the force and frequency of these eruptions. Where, we ask ourselves, is all this anger and hostility coming from? Is it normal for my child to be so easily provoked and aggressive, to speak so disrespectfully, to lash out over the tiniest things—or nothing at all?

The answer, sadly, is no. A happy child with strong self-esteem and an optimistic outlook is *not* so quick on the draw; she's more likely to empathize with others and can apply better problem-solving skills to frustrating situations. So if you or your caregiver or your child's teachers have felt the heat of your child's anger more than just occasionally, there is indeed cause for concern.

Anger itself is not always the demon emotion others have made it out to be; children can and should be allowed to react angrily to injustices, just as adults do. But while it is not always inappropriate for a child to be angry, it is never appropriate for a child to be mean. An angry child tends to react to everyday disappointments in a way that *is* inappropriate—and brings discomfort to those around her.

Many things can cause a child to misbehave or act unkindly toward others. He may be frustrated, lonely, overwhelmed, or suffering some hurt feelings. The anger may stem from family problems (such as divorce, alcoholism, death in the family), social problems (loneliness, teasing from peers), school problems (learning difficulties, underachieving), or internal problems (such as depression). The anger can be a reaction to stress in the overwhelmed family, or can be the way the child learned to act in order to get what she wants.

Every parent has had to face an angry child at one time or another; an angry outburst is a common reaction to life's troubles. How a parent deals with this anger can mean the difference between raising a confident and pleasant child or an insecure and ornery one. And stemming the tide of anger before it becomes an engrained response to any adversity or friction that arises, can make the difference between a home that is happy and one that is fraught with tension and animosity.

Perhaps you feel (or hope) your child's angry behavior is just a phase that will disappear in time. Sadly, this is unlikely to be the case. In my experience anger is an emotion that generally grows stronger over time. Left unaddressed, it can lead to more serious problems, even violence. It can be a corrosive force within a family that harms not only the child herself, but those around her. For this reason, it's important to identify anger as early as possible and lay the groundwork for change at once.

In my practice, parents often ask me how they can tell if their child's angry behavior is within a normal range or is truly cause for concern. I tell them to ask themselves the following questions:

■   ■   ■

As a parent:

- Do you feel caught in a vicious cycle of shouting or resorting to threats in order to get good behavior from your children and achieve peace in your home?
- Do you dread your child's reactions when you correct him?
- Do you lack confidence in your ability to defuse your child's tantrums or teenage tirades?
- Does your child make threats when she doesn't get her way?
- Does it seem that you're often picking up the pieces in the aftermath of your child's anger?
- Do you feel exhausted by daily struggles such as homework, bedtime, and chores you have assigned?
- Do you feel intimidated by your child, even avoiding interactions you know will be unpleasant?
- Do you sense an underlying anger about family problems (marital difficulties, alcohol or drug problems, rage, domestic violence, depression)?

Now, switch your thought process a bit. Does your child:

- Intentionally instigate conflict with unpleasant outcomes?
- Ignore requests or rules in order to frustrate the adults in his life?
- Provoke classmates, siblings, or others to battle?
- Refuse any responsibility for her outbursts, blaming everyone else?
- Whine or complain about the consequences or predicament his anger has landed him in?
- Have a difficult time understanding his own feelings, let alone how others may feel?
- Go into the attack mode whenever things don't go his way?
- Seem unaware of her own anger?
- Keep others at a distance with barbs, aggression, defiance, or with-holding?
- Use anger to manipulate an outcome to his advantage?
- Continue an argument way past its logical end?
- Make sweeping, negative generalizations, such as "everybody's a jerk," "all my teachers hate me," or "I can't do anything right"?
- Have difficulty solving problems except through intimidation, threats, and angry outbursts?
- Act nice when it serves her purposes, despite being angry at other times?
- Seem overly interested in violent music or television, video or computer games?

If you answered yes to some of these and feel beaten down by the vehemence of your child's unhappiness and ire, there is hope in the pages that follow. Know that the black cloud that seems to hover over your family is *not* a figment of your imagination. Such strong anger takes a heavy toll on all those who must coexist with the angry child, whether as caregiver, sibling, parent, or classmate. Fortunately, once understood, the acquired responses of the angry child can be unlearned and replaced with more constructive, kinder behaviors that will serve your child throughout her entire life. I don't promise overnight change, nor do I want to mislead you that the changes will be easy—for you *or* your child. I do promise that a less charged atmosphere and a more easygoing child will make your efforts very worthwhile.

When Does Anger Cross the Line?

A key first step in dealing with your child is to understand his anger in terms that help define what you are struggling with, which will empower you to take more effective action. Not all children with anger are "angry children." Learning to distinguish between the two is the first step toward helping a child gain control of his anger.

At times, Rachel resented her ten-year-old son Michael for the disdainful, disrespectful way he treated her, and she confided that she feared his verbal abuse would soon escalate to physical violence. She never knew when he was going to lose his temper or how far his threats and insults would go. It reached the point where she dreaded the sound of the school bus bringing him home from school. Each time it stopped at her house, her heart pounded heavily and her head ached.

On the other hand, Michael could be caring, affectionate, and lovable, especially to outsiders. Since he was able to control his anger with them, she hoped he would eventually come around if she tried her hardest to avoid unpleasantness and please him. Sadly, the opposite had proven true. Lately, Michael had been threatening to punch her, and once told her he'd dreamed that he was going to kill her. Rachel walked on eggshells in her own home, afraid to make any move lest her son pounce on her.

Claire, on the other hand, was a very bright child who seemed happy most of the time. She was a favorite with teachers and charmed her doting grandparents. But whenever her parents had guests over, she acted aloof and disdainful, refusing to make eye contact or answer questions. If they offered her a gift she would discard it scornfully. Although only five, her contemptuous attitude was cutting, and it caused her parents great embarrassment. Claire was also selfish, insisting other children watch her play with her toys rather than sharing them, and got irritated when her companions became bored and wandered off. At the table, she displayed the manners of a much younger child, and would spit food or fling it around if corrected by her mortified mother.

Angry children like Michael and Claire intimidate or embarrass their parents and caregivers and hold their homes in the grip of their anger. The lives of some are filled with tantrums and fights, while others direct subtle barbs and sarcasm at those around them. Some angry kids criticize constantly and are difficult to please. Verbal and physical threats are common, as are actual attacks on themselves and others. An angry child even attacks the people he loves by making nasty remarks to family and friends, as well as strangers. When the attack is aimed inward, it may show itself in the form of guilt, shame, or depression. One sees this in the child who withdraws from friends and family, or, in the worst cases, contemplates suicide.

But troubled children also show their anger by doing nothing at all. They may ignore requests to take care of chores or homework. Angry children may also have wide swings in their behavior, ranging from mean outbursts to sweet apologies. When their anger erupts, it may be so frightening to parents that it prevents them from responding appropriately.

Angry children can be masters of manipulation. They can use their anger with precision to keep parents at a distance or to get what they want. Like a chameleon, such a child may reveal her anger only to a select few. Outsiders may see her as an angel and find it hard to believe that little Mary could be the monster her parents describe. Teachers are often surprised to hear that their model student acts like the devil at home.

What is common among families with angry children is that they find living with these kids emotionally draining. When parents feel overwhelmed by their child's anger, when that anger seems a way of life, the child has crossed the line from just feeling angry to being an angry child.

In my own life, my legislative responsibilities often keep me away from home, and from my daughter. She knows I spend my mornings, afternoons, and nights helping others, but I can hardly blame her for being upset when I can't be there to help with her homework. I try whenever possible to be there for her, so that years from now she won't turn away in anger because I wasn't around when she needed me. It is a constant tugging of priorities. I have to remind myself continually that what I say and do are lessons to my daughter.

Not only do we model behavior by our time commitments to our children, but by our own anger management. That's why more vocal parents need to rein in the urge to yell. In such a house, everyone will surely need a hearing aid if the cycle isn't stopped. Since children depend upon their parents for safety and stability, watching Mom or Dad lose it is not only poor modeling, but scary. Kids are copycats. They'll mimic us as well as their playmates.

Similarly, the family that suffers in silence would be better served to communicate their feelings through open, honest discussion, lest they fall into or perpetuate a pattern of passive aggression. In homes where some silently harbor their wrath, the other family members don't even understand the reason for their anger. It just simmers.

A New Definition of Anger

It's apparent that there are real problems with the way people in general have come to express their anger and deal with anger in others. Our challenge is to start all over, rediscovering what anger is and what we can do about it. To this end I have developed a new definition of this age-old word.

According to *Webster's New World Dictionary*, anger is defined as "a feeling of displeasure resulting from injury, mistreatment, opposition, etc., and usually showing itself in a desire to fight back at the supposed cause of this feeling."

With all due respect to Webster, my goal is to redefine the anger in such a way as to give you a basis for taking action to defuse and control it. Here's my definition: *A powerful response, triggered by another negative emotion, that results in an attack of variable intensity that is not always appropriate.* Several keys to understand the roots of anger and how best to address it are embedded in this definition. Let's break it down:

1. Anger is powerful

Anger is a powerful, intense emotion. It has power over the child who becomes angry as well as his victims. An otherwise thoughtful child will become irrational in the grip of anger. A kind child may become cruel. When allowed to rage, anger takes over and blinds a child from experiencing other, more positive or rational thoughts and feelings.

Because anger is such a powerful emotion, it seems to cry out for an equally powerful response. A parent may also feel that the only way to get a child to respond is to become angry in return, fighting fire with fire. When kids obey, it convinces both the parent and the child that anger is the answer. But like any form of power, it must be exercised to maintain its potency. Parents yell more and more because their children no longer absorb gentle reminders. Conversely, kids reason that Mom doesn't mean business unless she screams. And an angry child quickly learns that if you really want something, you must shout to get it. When this vicious cycle spirals out of control, the home becomes a war zone, or worse.

Conversely, anger can intimidate. The parent of an angry child may try to avoid upsetting her because they have come to dread or fear the ugly aftermath of opposition. This is unlikely to erase the child's anger, however.

2. Anger is triggered by something

Anger is not a pure emotion. It doesn't exist in a vacuum. A broad range of negative emotions trigger anger—pain, frustration, loneliness, boredom, fear, rejection, jealousy, disappointment, embarrassment, depression, and humiliation, to name just a few. Each of these emotions can be dealt with more effectively than can the anger it engenders. As we'll see, most angry children are not cognizant that these trigger feelings even exist. Their swift and extreme reaction to negative feelings overshadows any recognition of a trigger. They go right to the anger without noticing that they're frustrated or disappointed. In fact, they may deny having these other feelings because the strength of their response blinds them to the buildup.

Learning to recognize these trigger feelings can help the angry child improve his self-control. When parents know what triggers their child's anger and cut the anger off at the pass, they can respond to the child more appropriately.

3. Anger is an attack

Unlike depression or hatred, anger is an active emotion that is invariably directed at someone, something, or even at oneself. An angry child doesn't just sit back. He fights back. The most obvious result takes the form of verbal threats, insults, or physical violence. When the anger is directed inward, however, you may see depression, school failure, or reckless or dangerous behavior.

4. Anger varies in its intensity

A wide spectrum of responses can be recognized as anger. It may manifest itself as a stamped foot, a frown, a thrown toy, or shouts of "I don't like you anymore." Or it may appear as screamed threats, an overturned school desk, smashed windows, arson, or physical attacks against family, friends, or teachers. It may come in the form of silent refusal to pick up toys, or sarcastic humor with a hidden agenda. Anger's intensity has an impact upon the target of the anger, to be sure. But there is also an impact upon the child himself. A young child, still immature in his development, may be frightened by his own overreaction to a problem.

Everyone's favorite neighbor and fellow Pittsburgher Fred Rogers often sings a song with the opening line: "What do you do with the mad that you feel when you feel so mad you could bite?" When children are young and growing, whether we're talking about a preschooler or a preteen, they aren't well equipped developmentally to deal with problems the first time around. The emotions a child experiences at not getting picked for the team or being rejected by the object of a crush are intense at these ages. That intensity is frightening to a child, who feels he must combat it with an equally intense reaction of his own.

5. Anger is not always appropriate

At times anger may seem appropriate and normal. Other times, it's absurd and immature. A basketball coach who is upset over a bad referee call in the final minute of a tied championship game may be excused for his anger, as long as his actions stay within reason. On the other hand, a four-year-old child who throws her food across the kitchen because she can't watch television will surely meet with disapproval.

Since anger is often confused with other feelings, the anger may not fit the problem at hand. Getting mad at his parent because his girlfriend broke up with him isn't appropriate, although we can empathize with his pain. If a child gets angry when his sister intentionally breaks his toy, we may understand the anger. But if that same boy breaks his own toy, then turns and hits his sister, he is misdirecting his anger.

There are also times when the inappropriateness is revealed in the power of his reaction. Is it okay for a child to rip up a test he just flunked and throw it on the teacher's desk? Should a teenage girl be excused for screaming at her ten-year-old brother who accidentally embarrassed her in front of a date? Just because we understand why the child became angry, we don't have to accept his reaction. Kids need to learn to control their responses.

To decide if the anger is appropriate, look at the intensity of the reaction and at whom it is aimed. Whose fault was it that he flunked the test? Did he study? Did a teacher or parent pressure him unduly? Regardless of the answer, it's never appropriate for a child to show disrespect for an adult. Remember: It's sometimes okay to be angry, but it's never okay to be mean. Every angry reaction to a difficult situation has a line that separates the acceptable from the unacceptable. Knowing where that line is drawn will help parents handle discipline and help children learn the boundaries of good behavior.

Not All Anger Is Bad

Anger can be a helpful emotion if it motivates us to take appropriate action to stop pain. The girl who gets angry enough to tell schoolmates to stop teasing her, or the boy who finally takes a stand against a bully, are prime examples of righteous anger. The same righteous anger could be expected when a parent has a pattern of missing a child's school events, after promising to be there. Who wouldn't be angry? But inappropriate anger is always counterproductive and leads to further escalation of a problem.

In response to a child's many frustrations, anger is normal. "How come he gets to do that and I don't?" is a reflection of sibling jealousy. Anger can also reflect frustration over not being able to do work or perform as well as expected. We've all seen the child who gets angry because her homework is too hard, or after the disappointment of losing an important ball game. In such cases anger is a reflection of a child's desire to do better and may well be one way she motivates herself to achieve more and do her best. But even in these circumstances there is a point at which anger may cross the line from being helpful to being hurtful. If the anger leads the child to blame others for his failures ("The coach and the team are stupid!") or to attack himself, rationalizing "what's the use . . . I'm just too stupid to do this," the anger has become destructive.

Similar reactions of anger foster the healing process after the death of a family member, friend, or a pet, as well as other losses, the breakup of a relationship, or the moving away of a friend. In these cases, anger is a signal that the child has not yet come to terms with the loss. These children need support and caring so they can move on with life. An angry child is often unaware of his emotions. His anger is a signal that he still needs help—help to understand his anger and help to recover from that pain. In such cases anger can again be productive, reminding a parent (who may himself be grieving or hurt) to attend to his child's needs.

Anger can also be a healthy step in coming to terms with an insurmountable problem. A story attributed to South African leader Nelson Mandela illustrates this point beautifully. As Mandela walked out to freedom, released after twenty-seven years in prison, he found himself feeling overwhelming anger at the guards who had controlled his life for over a quarter of a century. Then he had an insight: If he held on to his anger, these guards would still be controlling his life. Letting go of his anger is what gave him real freedom.

Here's another example of productive anger. For several months after an auto accident that left his legs paralyzed, an eight-year-old boy was constantly angry at the world. His parents also harbored angry emotions at the loss of their healthy son and the major change it meant in all of their lives. But with time and a good deal of thinking and talking, they were able to see that their anger wasn't going to improve their circumstances. They learned to view their situation not as a reminder of what was forever lost, but as a challenge that they could and must embrace in order to grow. They came to see that the value of having a family was greater than anything they had lost. They focused their energies on becoming stronger not *despite* the loss, but rather *because* of the loss. Their son's disability was a catalyst for the growth of their faith in and love of one another.

Of course, while we're discussing whether anger is appropriate or not, we need to touch on possible biological causes. Anger can stem from medical problems. Brain injury and neurological problems can both be manifested as anger and rage. Mood swings may accompany changes in blood sugar levels in diabetic children. Medications can also contribute to irritability and anger. Even allergies can sap a child's energy and ability to deal with problems in a calm manner. It's important to have your child checked by a pediatrician or family physician if you suspect a medical cause for the child's angry reactions.

Parents or educators who sense there could be an underlying chronic mood disorder will want to read Chapter 5, where childhood depression is discussed in greater detail. Children with attention deficit disorder may have particular problems with mood swings and controlling their behavior. In any case, consulting with your child's doctor is an essential part of dealing with the angry child.

Getting to the Root of the Problem

Before we can respond to a given child's anger, we must look deeper. With so many potential causes, there is no single, proper response. Just as diagnosing a disease properly indicates what medicine is needed, knowing the story behind the anger helps a parent act more effectively to defuse it. Often it is difficult to discern the reason behind a child's taciturn behavior. Is the anger a reaction to a recent issue that set the child off? Is it a tantrum over not getting a toy? Was she hurt and frustrated by taunting from classmates? Was he sad or depressed because a close friend recently moved away? Is your family experiencing marital problems? Do you have unrealistic academic expectations for your child and criticize her performance unfairly? Did a relative or other cherished loved one suddenly pass away? Is he struggling with schoolwork? The answers to these questions will influence how parents should react to their child and help them keep the angry feelings in check.

Angry reactions to troubled times are understandable. A child's anger is like a barometer reflecting the volatility of family storms. Pain in a child's life can lead to an angry cry for protection and security. But anger can take on a life of its own. Although it may stem from family frustrations, it can develop into an angry personality where the rage itself becomes a source of destruction in the family.

When a child feels angry and doesn't know what to do with that anger, it will gnaw at her and harm her in the form of tension, insomnia, lack of appetite, and headaches. It can affect every relationship that is important to her, and ultimately limit her prospects for happiness and success later in life.

Don't wait until your child is punching you, harming himself, or injuring friends to take action regarding his anger. It's much easier to put out a small fire in a frying pan than the blaze that's engulfing the house. Same thing with your child's anger. And note that anger in more subtle forms needs to be extinguished.

It's not easy, and it may require some uncomfortable soul searching on both your parts. But once you realize you don't have to live in the house of anger, these changes will look far less daunting.

Chapter Two

The Four Stages of Anger

W HEN CHILDREN explode in anger, even adults can feel intimidated and overwhelmed by the strength and depth of their emotion. We may also feel there is little we can do to stop or control the situation. Fortunately, this is not true. Every angry outburst follows a predictable progression from buildup to explosion through a series of four stages, and the good news is that each stage provides an opportunity for derailing the child's anger once you've learned to recognize it.

Witness a grouchy child whose anger simmers at a low level all afternoon, only to culminate in a fight when his sibling calls him a name. This name-calling may go back and forth for several minutes until it finally erupts into a knockdown battle. Another day the anger may strike with the swiftness of lightning, seemingly without provocation. Anger is often not a momentary event, but a process, sometimes starting days, months, or even years before a blowup. Sibling squabbles can last well into the teen years or

■ **Avoid situations that cause unnecessary frustrations.** Don't keep the kids up late if you know they won't have a chance to sleep in the next day. Why ask him to eat spinach if he's told you for eight years he doesn't like it? Don't buy her a pet she'll be responsible for if she's not mature enough to take on the job. If he's hungry, give him a snack. If she cannot handle long shopping trips, make them shorter.

■ **Know the normal developmental challenges for children so you can guide your child appropriately.** Each age presents its own problems. If you know what your child is going through, you can offer her the support she needs. Preschoolers may need more time to finish a meal. A nine-year-old may need to be shown how to do a chore once or twice before doing it alone. And a thirteen-year-old, despite her statements to the contrary, still needs to be hugged.

■ **Know your child.** Do you know your children's friends? Their families? Who is she talking to on the Internet? How does he spend his free time? Is she eating right? Getting enough sleep? Facing tough times at school? Knowing the answers to these questions allows you to deal with potential problems early.

■ **Teach your child how to talk over and solve problems.** Use the strategies described in Chapter 7 to help him identify problems and focus on solutions. Reinforce the strategies by demonstrating them in family situations. Tell them how you successfully handled problems you faced as a child.

■ **Establish an atmosphere of respect and caring in the home.** Show by your own example and by setting family standards that you expect everyone to respect the others' rights.

■ **Never, *ever*, put down or demean a child.** If he doesn't know how to do his homework, show him; calling him stupid or lazy is only going to build up his anger, lower his self-esteem, and teach him to treat you with equally harsh words when he gets angry.

■ **Follow through on discipline with fairness and consistency.** This includes applying the discipline methods described in Chapter 8 as well as understanding that some situations do not merit discipline at all.

■ **Choose your battles.** Some misbehavior needs to be corrected or punished right away. But in some cases, you're better off dealing with a child's immediate physical or emotional needs than focusing on punishment. The cranky child in the mall may need rest and a snack before she can learn anything from a time-out.

■ **When in doubt, follow the Golden Rule.** Treat your child with the same respect with which you would like to be treated.

■ **Build strong family bonds.** Do things together, enjoy each other's company, and keep relationships strong with relatives and friends. Parents with heavy work schedules, and divorced families, need to pay special attention to this.

■ **Maintain positive values in your family.** Choose books and movies that build confidence and healthy attitudes as well as good moral development. Set limits on their television and music. Avoid demeaning and aggressive themes and compliment positive ones. As a parent, choose the values your children will be exposed to, and actually teach them.

■ **Be aware of your own needs.** We all have our own stresses and disappointments to deal with. Prevent buildups by not taking these out on your child. Remember, she is not your therapist, or your whipping post. Don't vent your frustrations about work, your own childhood, or your marriage to her. Don't ask your child to take sides in arguments against your spouse or your boss. If you need help, get help from friends, trusted adults, or a therapist. Ignoring your problems or playing them out through your child only strengthens the foundation of your child's anger when he sees you carrying these unhappy feelings around with you, and contributes to a buildup of anger.

Stage Two: The Spark

The spark is the action or thought that sets off the angry outburst. It may be big or small. It can be a thought, a feeling the child experiences, or an action by someone else. Kids respond differently to potential sparks. Some may react with rage, while some may have no reaction at all.

The experiences in the buildup will influence how a child responds to a particular spark. For example, a spark may set off mild selective anger directed at a friend with whom there is no problematic history. Thus, a couple of six-year-olds may give each other the cold shoulder one moment and be ready to play the next. On the other hand, the spark could ignite a major rage between a parent and child who have a long history of mutual antagonism. If a parent and child have had countless arguments over using the telephone, its ringing during dinner may spark an argument. A child who feels she's had enough nagging about how she dresses may unleash a tirade in response to her father's innocent question "Are those new shoes?"

Think of the sparks that start nuclear meltdowns in your house. Common ones include "clean your room," "go to bed," "turn off the TV," "finish your dinner," "you cannot wear that," or "I won't buy you this today." Other external sparks may include being ignored by a friend, teasing, stubbing a toe, or getting caught in the act of breaking a rule.

It's important to recognize that it's not always an external event that sparks anger. Thoughts can also ignite an angry reaction, taking parents by surprise as their child seems to start a fight for no reason at all. Sixteen-year-old Adelle called to tell her mother she was on her way home. In the ten minutes it took her to drive home, her mood turned black; once in the house, she began to yell at her startled mother, complaining about what she'd served for dinner and claiming she couldn't stand it there another minute. Another parent recalls her five-year-old son Ben playing quietly on the couch while his three-year-old brother across the room looked at a book. Ben climbed off the couch, walked over and slugged his brother. "What happened?" she asked me. "Was there anything I could have done?"

Each child had probably reviewed a mental checklist of grievances that had festered for some time. Adelle may have been angered about having to leave her friend's house before she wanted to, or suddenly remembered an embarrassing comment her mother made long ago. Ben might have been thinking about how his brother took his toy the day before. Thinking about a problem was all it took to spark an angry reaction.

Children set off their own internal sparks with memories of being wronged by a teacher, spurned by a girlfriend, or by dwelling on their own failures. The thoughts don't even have to be about real events— their imaginations can create problems where none exists in reality. Immature reasoning skills can lead to the creation of illogical conclusions. A child can distort history when he gathers one memory from here, another from there, links them together, and presto! He's managed to create a whole new reality, in which he plays the unlucky victim. In such cases it's the parent's role to point out the faulty reasoning in a calm, nonjudgmental way, and douse the spark.

Because it can set off a firestorm of harsh words or actions, it's hard to ignore the event that sparks an outburst. But it's important that we don't mistake the spark for the problem itself. By falling into that trap, we run the risk of trivializing the child's anger and thereby missing the point. Think of the child who gets in a shouting match when told it's time for bed. Her reaction seems out of proportion to the situation. But what was the buildup that preceded the spark? Was she thinking about ways her parents baby her? Had she left homework undone that would earn her a reprimand in school? Does she get to stay up an extra half hour if she has a tantrum? Is she tired from having stayed up too late the night before? Look beyond the meaning of the moment and you will often find guidance for how to douse the spark.

Whereas during the buildup stage your goal was to prevent the problem, during the spark stage your goal is to *defuse* the problem.

- **Show respect.** Don't ever insult, tease, nag, or hit your child in anger. Meanness on your part makes everyone angrier, is a poor model for your child, and encourages her to associate anger with an attack.

- **Be reasonable.** Avoid absurd threats that set off further explosions and convince your child you're completely out of control and unfair. Don't say, "That does it, you're grounded for the rest of the year!" Instead say, "You still have to clean up your clothes before you can go to the ball game."

- **Listen.** Your child might be angry out of frustration over not being heard. If he says, "Why won't you ever just listen to me for a minute?" maybe you should do just that.

- **Walk away and cool off.** It's better to retreat and regroup than for both of you to hurl insults at each other. If you've lost your temper, tell your child you need time to calm down, then walk away and do something to relax. Do not, however, neglect to come back to the issue when you've cooled off.

- **Separate the actors.** If you're dealing with arguing siblings, send each to his room. Send other family members to another room, so they don't get drawn into the conflict as either victims or perpetrators. When I'm working with angry families in my office, I often have to talk to each one separately.

- **Label the correct feeling.** Once the explosion erupts, you may get a better sense of what your child is feeling. If your child is dealing with a painful experience, don't rob him of the right to that feeling. At times, a few well-placed words of understanding and empathy can stop an explosion in its tracks. Don't say, "You're just mad because no one wants to play with you." Do say, "I'm so sorry. I know that must really hurt a lot."

- **Avoid getting caught in argument traps.** Families, especially those in which arguments are commonplace, tend to fall back on such techniques as throwing in everything but the proverbial kitchen sink, tossing out a poison pill, or presuming to know what the other person is thinking or feeling. Other traps are pitting

Mom against Dad or playing the martyr. None of these helps bring about a fair resolution. We'll look at them and other argument traps in Chapter 7.

Stage Four: The Aftermath

Although the explosion stage gets most of the attention, what follows is probably the most important stage in dealing with anger, and it's also the most overlooked. The aftermath is when parents and children can confront both the original problem along with any new ones that may have come from the explosion. Whether you've been through a minor skirmish or a major battle, there will be wounded feelings and other injuries to address. Take care of them now. Small outbursts almost inevitably will escalate to large ones if the underlying cause is ignored. Whatever is left unresolved becomes the buildup for the next angry outburst.

You should recognize that even the smallest problems can teach big lessons. In my practice, I came to recognize a particular kind of angry outburst that I call a "microburst." In weather terms a microburst is a small, sudden, and powerful storm of wind and rain. Though brief, these little storms can knock down trees and capsize boats. The term also aptly describes those quick but intense explosions of anger that may end as quickly as they start. Often they happen so unexpectedly that parents don't see the buildup or the spark, but the stages are still there. They tend to occur over insignificant little problems that you might be inclined to ignore, but it's important for parents to keep their eyes open for these microbursts. How you handle them can be great tools for teaching your family how to handle deeper conflicts.

Five-year-old Aaron was playing with blocks on the floor of my office, struggling to build a very ambitious tower and becoming frustrated (the buildup). His precarious positioning of the blocks eventually caused them to topple (the spark). When his building collapsed, Aaron kicked the blocks and let out a little scream (the explosion), and soon went back to playing (the aftermath). In many cases a parent might reasonably choose to forget the whole episode since it ended as quickly as it started. But since these microbursts were a daily occurrence that had ultimately alarmed his parents enough to seek help, we decided to use this opportunity to show Aaron how to handle problems. It was a teachable moment I didn't want to let pass. If I waited for a bigger outburst, he might be too angry to talk.

First, I labeled the situation with an emotion Aaron and I could work with. If I had simply asked, "Why are you angry?" I would have had to talk to his anger, and he would have had to come up with reasons to justify it. That wouldn't have helped either of us. I said, "That's frustrating when the blocks fall down." He agreed and asked if I could show him how to build a tower that would not fall. While building a more stable tower, I mentioned how it can be difficult to build with blocks, and even intentionally let them fall a couple of times so I could model a more positive reaction. "Whoops," I said. "That didn't work. Maybe we should try it another way." We experimented with a number of techniques. I also calmly mentioned how I felt sad when he kicked my blocks, since I did not want my toys broken nor did I want him getting hurt. So I added, "I have to tell you about a rule. I'm happy to let you play with my blocks, but if you kick them again, they'll be put away." Finally, I redirected his feeling back to a positive mood by saying how fun it was to play with him.

In this brief aftermath interaction, I sent Aaron several messages. He learned (1) to relabel his feelings from anger to frustration, (2) how to solve a problem, (3) about my feelings, (4) what was expected of his behavior (the rule), and (5) what would happen if he broke the rule (the consequence).

If you have a child whose outbursts are more like prolonged hurricanes, this example might seem trivial. But bear in mind it's easier to teach the lessons of anger control on a small scale before attempting big problems. Parents often want to focus on the big problems, but those issues may be too burdened with emotions to allow a clear discussion. If you've got an angry child, start with solvable problems and build on these successes.

Your actions in this stage should address both the underlying cause of the problem and deal with the aftereffects of the explosion itself. Thus, in the aftermath stage, your goal is to solve the problem.

■ **Don't ignore the problem.** Just because the explosion is over doesn't mean the problem is solved. If something was big enough to lead to one explosion, then it's big enough to require your help. Otherwise, whatever led to it before will rear its ugly head again. As the parent, you're responsible for taking the lead to solve it. Letting it slide teaches that anger doesn't matter. If you're not sure what to do, or if the explosion was particularly severe, then get help. Talk it over with someone objective and who is trained to handle problem behavior in children.

■ **Debrief.** Angry kids avoid talking about problems. Talk anyway so you can gain more insight into the explosion. Imagine looking at a videotaped replay. To begin with, take a moment alone to write down the exchange as closely as possible with everything you or your child said or did. What else contributed to the blowup? Were you rushing? Did it occur in front of an audience? Did you hurl an insult? Were you hurt about something your child said that made you feel like retaliating? Recording the facts honestly will help you discover what contributed to the anger, both his and yours. How would you handle it differently? After you debrief with yourself, do the same with your child. Don't rekindle the argument by raising more accusations, threats, and insults. Debriefing steps back from a situation, looks upon it objectively, and says, "What went wrong here and how could we have solved it differently?"

■ **Pay attention to a teachable moment.** As minor as the incident may seem, and as much as you might like to move on, step back to review it and dissect it—calmly and briefly—with your child.

■ **Hold a family meeting to solve the problem.** Do this especially if you promised to talk it over later when everyone calmed down. Though the actual topic may never come up again, you will establish better ways to handle future issues. (See Chapter 7 for rules regarding family meetings.)

■ **Follow through on discipline.** Even if you have worked to deal with whatever set off the anger, you may still need to follow through. Remember, it's okay to be angry but it's never okay to be mean. If your child was mean-spirited, he may need to be disciplined. Likewise, if you acted meanly, you need to address this with your child. If the house rule holds that everyone has to pay a fine each time something mean is said, pay up. On the other hand, if you blurted out a stupid or absurd discipline while angry, think it over. You gain nothing by following through on foolish threats such as "I will throw away all of your toys." If you made a mistake, admit it, retract it, and move on. This sends another important message—that you're mature enough to admit your mistakes.

■ **Keep loving your child.** After an explosion, especially a severe one, you might be tempted to withdraw your affection. Don't. Your love will provide the energy needed to handle the problem. Love motivates you to help your child. Anger, guilt, and resentment won't sustain your parenting energy. It's hard to hug someone who only an hour ago said some pretty nasty things, but affection can go a long way. The energy that comes from love will continue to warm your child long after the heat of her anger has run its course.

■ **Practice the right response.** The calm between storms provides the perfect opportunity to practice how you will handle the next conflict. After an angry blowout we often replay the bad parts of the argument in our minds. This keeps anger percolating and reinforces our tendency to act the wrong way. Instead, rehearse better ways to handle the conflict. Plan what you could say or do differently.

■ **Apologize.** If you said or did something wrong, this is the time to make your peace. The same expectation for an apology applies to your child. Bear in mind, however, that an apology does not make everything all right. Problems still need to be discussed and solved.

■ **Forgive.** There's nothing gained and much lost in holding grudges. Refusing to forgive leaves your own temper simmering, ready to explode with the slightest provocation. This doesn't mean you should forget what happened, as this would jeopardize your ability as a parent to be consistent, focused, and determined to help your child. Remember what your child said and did, recalling how you acted and reacted. Don't forget your goal to help your child grow and learn to control his feelings. Forgetting can let the wrong issues slide. Remember both the bright and harsh moments in order to focus your actions to bring out the best. Forgive but don't forget.

■ **Think again.** Sometimes in the face of anger, parents agree to things in hopes of pacifying their child. "I'll buy you something if you calm down" or "Okay, okay, you can take the car" can end up rewarding anger. So think again. Some parents feel they have to follow through on the argument pledge, or they'll provoke another outburst. Use your judgment to decide what's best in the calm aftermath. But if you do give in, use it as a learning experience so you don't give in to the threats next time.

The Four Stages of Anger in a Nutshell

Anger Stage	Contributing Factors	Your Goal	Suggested Action
1. The Buildup	· experiences · learned attitudes · past reactions · physical stress · low self-esteem · unrealistic attitudes · poor coping skills	Prevent an outburst	· deal with child's immediate need (nap, snack) · avoid unnecessary frustration · understand child development and needs · talk calmly · teach problem solving
2. The Spark	· mutual antagonism · sight/thought of something unpleasant · hot button words/ phrases such as "clean your room" or "eat your vegetables" · outside influences/ mishaps · immature reasoning	Defuse the problem	· look beyond the spark for the true problem · calm down and listen · label the correct emotion · offer a diversion, another activity, even a laugh · restate house rules
3. The Explosion	· raised voices · insults · name calling · physical action (grabbing, kicking) · subtle attacks such as silent refusal, hiding, or damaging property	Contain the explosion and minimize any resulting damage	· stay calm · don't bargain or threaten · remind of discipline · cool off · separate the actors
4. The Aftermath	· magnitude of the outburst · your degree of calm · your control of your own emotions · your expressions, forgiveness, apologies, continued love	· Resolve the problems · Gain insight to forestall future episodes	· talk over what happened · use teachable moments for problem solving · manage any microbursts · call family meetings · follow through on discipline

Chapter Three

Ten Characteristics
of the Angry Child

GROWING KIDS face challenges every day—
learning to walk, read, hit a baseball. Every
age is filled with situations that can foster a sense of
accomplishment or trigger anger. Life gets tough
and kids respond in kind. The infant is hungry, the
preschooler wants every toy she sees, or the preteen
is snubbed by peers and the frustration that erupts is
predictable. It's our job to anticipate problems and
offer proper responses.

Your child's unique personality adds another
dimension. One child may have a short fuse, while
another is more tolerant. A high activity level, impulsiveness, and a low tolerance for frustration lead
a child to react to conflict in a way very different
from a child with a more patient and calm temperament. These two ingredients—the qualities they
were born with and their experiences over time—
will influence each other for years.

Learning how to handle an angry child means you
have to understand how the child thinks. Parents

can feel a little lost when it comes to comprehending an angry child, but understanding some basic characteristics of angry children makes them better equipped to deal with the anger. This chapter explains what makes these kids so angry and why they stay that way.

Most children have the capacity to bounce back from difficult situations, fretting briefly over a setback and then moving on. But an angry child keeps the conflict flowing. Angry children can be gentle and sweet when not challenged, but they can turn a skirmish into a war that continues to simmer long after we wave the white flag. This in turn influences how parents and teachers react to that child, who soon finds that the world is filled with compliments for or complaints about his behavior. He starts to shape his own beliefs about how people are treated based upon these experiences. That child carries these thoughts and expectations into new situations. Thus, if he expects criticism, he can either change or fight back, sometimes in ways that don't make sense to an observer. Our goal is to help these children change, but first we need to understand what makes them the way they are.

The Angry Child's Traits

From working with hundreds of children, I've identified ten characteristics that shape the way an angry child views the world and handles adversity. This list explains why life with the angry child is so incredibly frustrating. Each characteristic may exist in varying degrees within each child. After learning the traits and how to work with each, parents often tell me, "I finally understand how my child thinks. Now I see why it's so difficult getting him to change."

1. ANGRY CHILDREN MAKE THEIR OWN MISERY
Have you ever heard your child say, "I can't help it . . . trouble just seems to follow me." In fact, angry children *do* make their own misery, often setting up situations that are bound to provoke angry reac-

Ten Traits of the Angry Child

1. Makes his own misery
2. Can't analyze problems
3. Blames others for his misfortune
4. Turns bad feelings into mad feelings
5. Lacks empathy
6. Attacks people rather than solves problems
7. Uses anger to gain power
8. Indulges in destructive self-talk
9. Confuses anger with self-esteem
10. Can be nice when they want to be

tions. They rarely initiate social situations that have pleasant outcomes, and are unaware that they create their own problems. In some cases they intentionally instigate a mess.

Furthermore, angry children see problems where there were none. Sometimes they light their own fuse, and sometimes they do nothing to extinguish those already burning. Either approach can set the stage for battle.

Often these children will profess ignorance and surprise when things turn ugly. One father told me of watching television with his eight-year-old son Patrick. After a while Patrick got up and went over to his two-year-old brother Daniel, who was playing quietly nearby.

"What do you have there?" Patrick asked Daniel, grabbing his toy away. The younger boy tried repeatedly to get his toy back, but Patrick held it out of reach. Eventually, Daniel started to scream, causing his father to lash out at Patrick.

"You're doing this just to annoy me!" the father shouted. "You can't stand to let me relax in peace."

"Doing what? I'm just playing," Patrick fired back. "Danny's the one screaming."

"You know darn well what you did. Now I want you to—" Jack cut his sentence off when he saw Patrick's eyes roll. "That's it! Get up to your room!"

"What did I do? You're always picking on me," Patrick muttered, stomping up the stairs. "I didn't want to be around you anyway."

Sometimes children actively cause problems; sometimes they cause them by doing nothing. Yet, this passive approach can be just as provocative. Seventeen-year-old Greg decided he was going to stop talking to his teachers since it usually led to an argument. Trouble was, he never told his teachers of his plan and he just seemed to be ignoring people. A teacher commented on his rude behavior one day, and before long Greg was back in the principal's office—without ever having uttered a harsh word.

Children like Patrick and Greg usually find battles even when they think they're avoiding trouble. When our expectations influence our actions, they can lead to the expected outcome. It's called a self-fulfilling prophecy. But we can change self-fulfilling prophecies. If we believe hard work and tenacity eventually pay off, despite failures or mistakes, we can succeed. It's a matter of adjusting our expectations. Our expectations also influence how others react to us. As adults we can see how employees will behave far differently for a boss who believes they are inept than for one who trusts they are competent.

Often, angry children have little or no insight into their role in a conflict even when they are so obviously the direct cause. They may rationalize why they reacted a certain way and fail to see how their grudges or tough-guy attitude could have led to conflict. For example, siblings use expectations to keep battles going for weeks, months, and years. They never seem to forget, using past events to justify their actions.

"Why did you take your sister's candy?" one mother asked her seven-year-old daughter.

"Because she took mine."

This mother was curious. "When did she take yours?"

"On Halloween."

"But Halloween was six months ago!" her mother exclaimed.

"She still took it. Why are you always taking her side?"

Adults can also play a part in these self-fulfilling prophecies. Research has found that a teacher's expectations are a powerful influence on a child's personality and intellectual growth. Teachers who believe a student is intellectually gifted may give him more attention, which in turn motivates learning. Likewise, when teachers label a child a troublemaker, they watch for problems and naturally see them. Their expectations magnify their perceptions. If peers, parents, and teachers expect to see anger, even the slightest grimace from the child leads them to say, "See, you just can't stop causing trouble." Expect to hear in return, "You're not fair. Other kids get away with this. Why are you picking on me?" And the battle continues.

In order to deal with angry children, we need to remind ourselves that these children have a knack for provocation. We need to take care that they don't get caught in their own self-fulfilling prophecies. When both the child and the adults go into an encounter braced for an argument, it's difficult to change the cycle. Parents and teachers can help break the cycle of expectations by dealing with each situation as a unique event. Avoid guilt by reputation. Make the rules in the home or classroom the same for each child. If your child needs discipline, mete it out only for the transgression at hand. Focus on fairness and relinquish the grudges. Give him room to change and announce an expectation that he can. Most of all, avoid negative labels of a child as they send the message that she cannot change for the better.

Instead, indicate that you are correcting your child because you know he *can* change. A focus on helping the child sets a more positive goal for action and change. Watch out for insults and demeaning phrases like "I don't know why I bother" or "You never listen anyway." A comment like "I know that you can change for the better, and I'm going to help you do just that" can reset the self-fulfilling prophecy in a positive direction. Teach children to avoid overgeneralizing. Parents can also be good role models by voicing positive

they may make untrue claims about parental actions, as they reconstruct the event in order to justify their own behavior.

Angry children also magnify the details that support their point of view. If the details don't fit, they forget them. For angry children, analysis of an angry outburst is not a process that incorporates new information. Rather, it takes them full circle right back to the assumption that provoked their anger in the first place. This circular thinking isn't logical, but in the mind of the angry child, it works, in that they change history in their mind to fit their conclusion that it's not their fault. When parents hear their child's version, they scratch their heads, wondering if they were at the same battle.

I recall a session with a ten-year-old named Stephen, who had a three-inch scratch across his face. When I asked what had happened, he said, "My brother scratched me."

I asked why, and Stephen replied, "He's a wimp. He has two-mile-long fingernails."

"But why did he scratch you?" I persisted.

"'Cause he's a wimp."

"Well, what did you do before he scratched you?"

"Nothing. He's a wimp."

I wasn't giving up here, but chose a different approach, asking, "What was happening just before he scratched you?"

"Me and my friend were teasing him because he *is* a wimp. He deserves it."

Do you see the circular thinking pattern? Stephen doesn't admit to provoking his brother. He focuses his story to justify his original opinion of his brother. As outsiders, we can see the absurdity of Stephen's explanation. Each time you try to get an angry child to rethink the problem, he starts with his conclusion and uses distorted thinking to circle back to support that conclusion.

How to help

Since the heat of the battle limits a child's ability to think, the middle of a tantrum is not the time to discuss a problem. Cool down before you talk and you both may be able to see the facts more clearly. Parents can be great role models in showing a child how to talk calmly. Also, teach thinking strategies over time that will allow a child to analyze arguments more effectively. What I've seen work best with the parents I advise is a three-pronged approach: gathering all the facts, showing children another point of view, and helping them to see how their actions lead to a fight or a solution. For example, when reading aloud or watching a movie, comment about the characters, how they are acting, and ask the child to anticipate what's going to happen next. Or, use board games (or chess/checkers) to teach her how to use logical problem-solving, anticipate errors, avoid mistakes, and calmly react to unexpected results. These little lessons add up over time to help children of any age gather facts and weigh them more clearly.

Parents can also teach by discussing real-life problems, on the child's level. Explain how you dealt with a disagreement with a mechanic over an auto repair bill. Let your child know how you remained calm (assuming you did) and solved the problem in a productive way. Sometimes the simplest solution can yield big results. I've asked kids to teach me how to draw pictures, sharpen a pencil, or explain their video games. All the time, I've pretended I didn't know how to do it as a mechanism to get them to learn to slow down and explain the steps to solving the problem. Silly? Maybe. But is it an effective way to build problem-solving skills? You bet!

Sometimes the child has trouble learning to solve problems because their parents do too. One family had a lot of trouble talking over issues with their child because Dad characteristically resorted to threats with his son. His son, in turn, would attack and threaten his father. Between the two of them, they were making things worse on a daily basis. Talking to this dad about the principles of child psychology was getting us nowhere, so I decided to play to the father's strengths by getting him to help *me* solve a problem.

At the end of one session, I switched to my senator's hat and asked for his advice on getting a bill through that a legislative leader and I were not agreeing on. At first this father suggested that I hold a press conference and attack the other guy's position, embarrass him in the newspapers, and force public opinion to change his mind. I explained to him how, first of all, I wasn't sure I was totally right or that this legislative opponent was totally wrong, and that the attack mode would only assure me that any bill I sponsored in the future would never move through the state legislature.

Dad thought for a second, then suggested I sit down and talk with some senate colleagues who also disagreed with me and get their honest feedback. "I've always found showing a little humility goes a long way toward building better relationships," he advised me.

"Sounds to me," I replied, "that you know what you've got to do with your son, then."

Feel-think

The third limitation on the angry child's thinking skills is his tendency to confuse feelings with facts. When a child operates under the assumption that an emotion is all the data he needs to draw a conclusion, he's engaging in what I call "feel-think." That is, he's assuming that his feelings alone justify a strong response or action—even if the reality of the situation doesn't support this reaction. Emotions have a powerful influence on our thinking. So powerful are feelings that people, especially children, will conclude they must be true.

Two eighth-grade boys, Jacob and Brian, were at their lockers. When a mass of Jacob's books crashed from the locker to the floor, he was embarrassed, and when Brian glanced over at the noise, Jacob grabbed Brian by the collar and snarled, "Who are you laughing at?"

"I'm not laughing at anybody, I was just—"

"You were laughing at me," Jacob insisted, convinced he wouldn't be embarrassed unless someone were laughing at him.

"Relax, Jacob. What makes you think anybody was laughing at you?"

"Because I'm mad and I wouldn't be mad if you weren't making fun of me."

Feel-think stood in the way of Jacob's ability to properly analyze the situation.

Adults can easily see how feel-think affects our reasoning. Positive and negative emotions can both cloud our thoughts. On the positive side, love can blind us with feel-think, as in, "Because I love you, you can do no wrong and must be perfect." But feel-think can also magnify destructive emotions like jealousy, as in, "If I feel jealous it must mean you are doing something behind my back." Experience and maturity give us the perspective to weigh these emotions against more objective truths.

Young children are at a disadvantage because they don't have the experience to know how to weigh their feelings. At its worst, feel-think prevents a child from ever moving beyond an emotional reaction to a more thoughtful, reasoned one. Anger energizes them for attack before logic can prevail.

Overcoming feel-think involves teaching the difference between feeling and thinking. It's important to show kids that their feelings may be based upon partial truth, and therefore lead them to a wrong conclusion. They should understand that two people can view the same situation in two different ways, and have different feelings about it as well—both of which are valid, neither of them more "right" than the other.

Try this simple exercise to show your child how different people can have different emotional reactions to the same things. Give him or her a list of words like tree, farm, city, soldier, kitten, gun, ice cream, homework, television, win, lose, marriage, divorce, teacher. Ask her to state the feeling that comes to mind when she thinks about each word. If you have more than one child, have them give you a response separately to each word. A spouse or your child's friends can also participate. Finally, compare the lists. Some feeling words may be similar, but others will illustrate this concept.

Another method is to use the plot from a child's book or movie to illustrate your point. A common theme in many plots includes characters that make mistakes because they don't have all the facts. Ask questions such as, "What's she feeling now?" and watch how the reaction changes with the discovery of more facts.

3. ANGRY CHILDREN BLAME OTHERS FOR THEIR OWN MISFORTUNE

Angry children see others as the cause of their anger. In other words, someone or something else provokes them, and anger is the only reasonable response. It's not their fault they lost their temper. By placing the blame elsewhere, they sidestep responsibility for their feelings and reactions, as well as the damage they cause.

Ten-year-old Heather made an agreement with her mom that she would keep out of fights with her parents for an entire week. On the first day of their pact, Heather came home bothered, having been teased at school. She entered the house, slammed the door, and stomped to her room. Her mother calmly asked, "Couldn't you even stay calm for one day?"

"I hate you all," Heather shouted back. "Even when I try to change there's nothing I can do. You all make me sick."

Children like Heather feel they have little control over their lives. They feel pain and get upset at those they believe cause that pain. They may conclude there's little they can do (outside of attacking others) to stop bad things from happening to them. This external blame increases their anger. Not only do they become angry at others, but they feel powerless to prevent problems.

Mary had few school friends, and often seemed to get in fights when she did have a rare play date. Eager to help her daughter forge some new friendships, Mary's mother invited a new neighbor to play dolls with Mary, cautioning her to try to play nicely.

The play date started off well enough, until the girls decided to put on a play with their dolls. Mary insisted her doll was the queen and that the other girl's doll must be the servant. "Can't she be the princess?" the other girl asked.

"No," Mary replied. "There is no princess."

When several other suggestions were shot down by Mary, her playmate lost interest in their play and asked to go home, saying she wasn't having fun. When Mary's mother asked what had gone wrong, Mary focused only on the girl's refusal to join in her game, glossing over her own refusal to compromise and her insistence that she alone take a starring role. She needed to own up to her own role in cutting short the play date, and cultivate better social skills.

Angry children bring trouble upon themselves with their interactions. They may talk to parents and peers with a sarcastic tone that grates and causes friction. They may criticize others frequently. They may adopt an in-your-face manner because they don't know when to back off. They may nag until a parent's patience snaps. Ironically, angry children seem unaware that their actions are provocative, and seem genuinely aggrieved that "everyone picks on them."

Sometimes, however, the child's sense of being victimized is right on the mark. In troubled families, children may rightly see that others are indeed to blame. When a child grows up in an alcoholic or abusive family, she may be justified in feeling there's nothing she can do to change the situation. A parent's abusive or cruel actions make the child's anger very understandable.

Even when there is a reason for a child's reactions, it does not absolve him of responsibility. There is a difference between an explanation and an excuse, but angry children often do not see the difference. Tracey was adopted by the stable and loving family who provided foster care for her during her first three years of life. When Tracey turned nine, she started acting resentful toward her adoptive parents with a rage that lasted for hours at a time. Counseling revealed her anger was with her biological mother and subsequent feelings of rejection and abandonment. She minimized her angry behavior with her parents, saying they had to put up with it since she was mad at her birth mother. "It's not my fault she left me," Tracey explained after one of her outbursts. This presented a heart-wrenching dilemma for her folks as they struggled between wanting to control her behavior, and empathizing with her very real emotional pain.

This family endured much discord before they came to a happy conclusion. How? By getting Tracey to understand she could work on her feelings toward her birth mother, while her adoptive parents set limits on her behavior. Years later, Tracey told me that when her parents enforced the rules it reminded her of their deep commitment to her. "I learned that no matter what I did, they were not going to abandon me, even though I tried my best to drive them away."

In such cases, an angry child may bring trouble with her. When children let anger fester long after the pain has stopped, problems multiply. They lash out at schoolmates and teachers who have nothing to do with their problems at home. Such a child needs to learn better ways of handling emotional stress (instead of attacking others), and learn that there are people who can be trusted—not everyone is to blame for their unhappiness. This is difficult for the angry child.

Whether another person may truly share the blame for a child's anger, the angry child will characteristically find a way to deflect the blame for the problems they generate. Everyone is suspect and no one is seen as the source of help unless they're in agreement with the angry child's blaming. With no one to turn to, the child's feelings of rage bubble below the surface, and it takes very little to trigger them.

Watching their effort to blame everyone else and avoid responsibility, I'm often struck how angry children avoid taking responsibility even for their *own* thoughts:

"One part of my brain tells me to stay calm and another part tells me to be angry," said a nine-year-old. "I can't help it if the angry side wins." His need to place blame allowed him to avoid responsibility for controlling his own mind, as if it were separate from the rest of him. These feelings of disconnection compound a child's stress and helplessness. Many children will say they couldn't help it after an angry outburst. They may seem to wash their hands of the situation, but these children are hoping for understanding. They don't comprehend their anger any more than we do, as spectators. Despite the tendency to blame others, children crave control over their feelings. They don't want to feel powerless.

Even when a situation clearly involves no fault, the angry child will still point the finger. Angry children mistake the meaning of accidents, and assume others do things on purpose to hurt or thwart them. If something happened, someone must have done it to be mean, they conclude. When in doubt, they interpret a situation as hostile and lash out. Maybe someone bumped into her in the hall at school, maybe the TV station interrupted his favorite show for a news bulletin. One young man I treated held his parents responsible when the phone line to his Internet service provider was busy.

In other cases, even when someone is trying to be nice, the angry child interprets it as antagonistic. When Chad's parents asked him about his day at school, he would shout back, "Quit prying into my business!" His parents didn't understand how such an innocent question could set him off, but Chad felt they were accusing him of using drugs or drinking even when his parents explained they weren't.

"Why do you always get so angry when we're just asking a simple question?" his parents would ask. Unable to respond to their concern, Chad snapped back, "If you know I'm gonna get angry, then you must ask just to get me mad." Again, the blame for the conflict was shifted away from himself.

This pattern of misinterpreting ambiguous situations looms large for the angry child's family. One mother recalled how she simply sat down at the kitchen table and let out a tired sigh. Her daughter, who had been watching television in another room, burst in screaming, "If I disgust you that much then why don't you just leave the house."

The blame surfaces this way, with the belief that "if I attack you, drive you away, you are no longer bothering me, and if I feel better then you must have been the source of my misery."

"I wasn't sighing because you disgust me," the mother explained. "I was simply tired. Please don't take it so personally."

But her daughter still might respond with, "Well, if it wasn't meant to be personal, why are you yelling?" If the argument ends here, neither one has an opportunity to find out what's going on, and the child may continue to feel justified in blaming. Unfortunately, assigning blame where there is none drives people away, including those who might help a child the most. A key to helping the angry child is to turn around the pattern of blaming.

Angry children must learn to distinguish between the genuinely hostile situation and the innocuous one where no harm is meant. The girl in the example above may have had a history of troublesome interactions with her mother or none at all. Perhaps she had a history of conflict with her father and lashed out at her mother instead. Who knows? If they talked, they might discover better ways to interact with one another.

How to help

Teach children to recognize the causes of the anger and suggest alternative resolutions to accusations. In your own behavior, avoid blaming and shaming words and actions—they're destructive and will only worsen the situation.

"Nothing is ever your fault," one father shouted to his daughter. "It's always the rest of the world. Never you!"

Although Dad's message may be accurate, it will only add to his daughter's anger.

This blaming creates an even wider chasm between the parent and child. It both adds to a child's feelings of helplessness and conveniently absolves her of responsibility for the confrontation. Best not to focus on placing blame when blame is the child's crutch you're trying to correct. If kids could take responsibility, of course things would be better. But if they already have a pattern of blaming, you can start by modeling a different approach. You may get more mileage out of saying, "Even if someone else is to blame, let's think of a way to handle it that helps *you*."

Also avoid pointless discussions of whether someone deserved what your angry child dished out. If you say, "I can understand why you stole his homework because he took yours before," you're teaching your child you condone meanness and blame. Whenever there is another solution, teach it. If you don't know of one, try and find one.

Don't worry if it takes time to find a solution. Patience is part of the lesson of problem-solving.

And regardless of the rationalization, if your child did something wrong, then it's wrong. Although there may be some exceptions to the rules, such exceptions should be rare. One may be excused for exceeding the speed limit en route to the hospital, but otherwise, a rule is a rule. We can be more tolerant of a child's anger when his feelings are hurt, but when he is being mean just to manipulate and intimidate, always enforce the rule.

4. FOR ANGRY CHILDREN, BAD FEELINGS BECOME *MAD* FEELINGS

In our definition of anger, you'll recall we said that anger is always associated with another negative emotion. Now, think of a child who has little sensitivity to understand those other feelings, and you have the next important characteristic of the angry child: they very often misinterpret their negative feelings.

Once labeled as anger, it's difficult for children to accept that another feeling may have triggered their ire. This is why when you ask an angry child how she feels about different situations, she'll use the same one-word answer each time: "Mad!"

The angry child often acknowledges only one negative emotion in his world—anger. Fear, confusion, embarrassment are transition emotions or the way to the final destinations—anger and attack. If the angry child were able to label the *real* feeling that prompts his action, other possibilities would emerge. A child frustrated by a difficult project might try a new approach or take a break. An intimidated child could ask his dad how to handle the bully basketball player in gym class. But when the child feels only the anger, he acts only on the angry impulses.

I've seen this again and again in my practice when I try to help a patient find a label other than the word "mad" for his list of various scenarios. On one occasion, I asked a nine-year-old child how he felt when his sister gave him a present. When he replied that it made him mad, I said, "Wait a minute. She just gave you a present, and you're mad?"

"Well, she probably didn't buy it. Mom did," the boy said.

Even when I presented a couple of other possibilities for how he'd feel, the boy wouldn't budge. "I'd still be mad," he said. "'Cause when she's around, she makes me mad." As he went on to describe the situation in greater detail, I was able to help this child see that he had feelings of rejection, jealousy, and frustration that caused him to be mad at his sister. Since he didn't understand his own trigger emotions, it was hard to get him to move beyond his anger. Add into the mix the characteristic of feel-think and resistance to talking over problems, and you can see why it's so difficult to get the angry child to change and react in less aggressive, violent ways when confronted with negative emotions.

How to help

Parents can help immensely by simply labeling their child's feelings correctly. Granted, this is tough when you have a child yelling at you, but by using the right label, you may actually dissolve the anger. Even a validating "That must be terribly disappointing for you" draws the child's attention to a feeling she can control versus the anger that clouds her ability to deal with the original trigger. The trick for the parent is discerning the true trigger feeling.

Psychologists have often encouraged parents to label children's feelings only as anger, telling them, "You must be angry," and leaving it at that. This response makes the child more conscious that he is in the midst of a powerful emotion. If it helps him redirect the anger to take effective action, that's good, but if it only keeps him mired in anger, it serves little purpose. Besides, the angry child already knows he's mad. He needs help learning the feeling that triggered the anger. Saying "You must be angry" may adequately label the reaction feeling, but it obscures the trigger. By labeling only the anger, the parent prevents the child from recognizing his other emotions (thus maintaining a limited understanding of feelings).

Remember, anger doesn't exist in a vacuum. There is surely another emotion at work when a child has an angry outburst. But don't worry about attaching the perfect label. And even if you are correct, your child may resist or deny the label, protesting "I'm not jealous" or "I'm not being selfish." Just try to build everyone's awareness of feelings. You may make mistakes, but acknowledge them, be patient, and over time you'll both get better at it.

5. ANGRY CHILDREN LACK EMPATHY

Not only are angry children not very good at understanding their own feelings, they're lousy at understanding the feelings of others. They confuse other people's feelings.

A young patient named Kevin recounted an instance in which he'd made a relatively innocuous comment to his sister that caused her to burst into tears and earned him a reprimand from his mother. Kevin honestly had no idea why his sister was crying, when in fact years of merciless teasing had taught her to fear Kevin's veiled barbs. When his mother asked why he was still picking on her, he said, "She's just crying to get me in trouble. I didn't do anything." Kevin refused to acknowledge that his teasing had brought his sister genuine pain. He honestly thought she was faking it. If he had cared about his sister's feelings, he might at least have tried to find out why she was crying. He might have felt guilty to learn she lived in fear of his taunts, and tried to stop tormenting her. But if he stopped, he would also lose his power over her, as well as his favorite punching bag, which was ultimately more important to him than his sister's emotional state.

Just as anger can blind a child, it can also keep a child from recognizing someone else's feelings. Because of their age and developmental stage, children already have difficulty understanding how others feel. Preschoolers may have only an emerging sense of this. School-age children get better at it, but in a moment of rage, kids can lose all sensitivity to someone else. Kids need to understand that we *all* have feelings, and that just as we react to how others treat us, so too we can affect how others feel.

Children living painful lives often defend themselves from feeling overwhelmed by shutting down their sensitivity to others. This lack of empathy is part of a defensive wall children erect to keep from being hurt. Another part of that defense is anger that holds others at a distance through intimidation and fear.

At age eleven, Tony's wall was well reinforced. Years of being caught in the emotional tug-of-war between his divorced parents had left him numb. "For years, they never cared how I felt," he said "and now I don't care about how they feel."

When children appear to lack sensitivity to another's feelings, it is of particular concern. In extreme forms, these children may have no qualms about torturing animals or hurting others. Luckily, these attitudes are rare, but if you see these signs in your child, it is important to discuss them with his doctor or another professional.

How to help

For most children, you can turn this problem around by improving their understanding of feelings and by making sure they have adults around whom they can trust.

With young children, you can make a scrapbook of feelings. Cut pictures from magazines with different facial expressions and have your child sort these into categories. Let them choose the labels for the feelings and make pages for each one. This will tell you the level on which your child is understanding emotions. Many angry kids will start out with a list of only three or four emotions, but you can enrich your child's sensitivity by increasing her emotional vocabulary. Try working with the following words: surprised, lonely, cheerful, frustrated, disappointed, laughing, puzzled, worried, afraid. Avoid the word "angry." Over time you'll add several dozen words. Your child will end up with an illustrated dictionary of new feelings to identify her own as well as other people's feelings.

Older children can be helped by encouraging them to write down stories in a diary or journal. When they are faced with a problem, ask them to write or talk about a description of what happened from the other person's point of view. Lastly, describing your own experiences can provide a powerful tool for emulation. Children of all ages will learn to empathize from hearing you talk about your own emotions when you faced (or continue to face) difficult situations.

6. ANGRY CHILDREN ATTACK PEOPLE RATHER THAN SOLVE PROBLEMS

Angry children have a very limited repertoire for dealing with upsetting situations. Their main response—their one weapon—is to attack, immediately or later. The angry child sees only anger in others and thinks attack is the only recourse. It's like the saying, "When your only tool is a hammer, everything looks like a nail." Since his aggression may scare people away or even get him what he wants, he assumes his anger solved the problem.

Every child confronts situations every day that could spark anger. Maybe he couldn't find his socks. Maybe someone tried to pick a fight with him at school. Maybe he felt a teacher wasn't being fair. Some children stay calm, while others snap. I've shown earlier that anger manifests as a physical or verbal attack toward another person, an object, or against oneself. The attack can be an insult or a provocative statement, or it can be silent refusal to complete a task. Angry children often view aggression and violence in more positive terms than other children. Whereas another child may choose to talk, seek help, or walk away, the angry child sees this as passive or weak; he prefers to go on the offensive. Power comes from the attack, and power is what angry children crave. Aggression is the power he uses to keep someone away or win an argument. Both fights and threats serve this purpose. But angry children also use aggression just for the sake of destruction, even if it's counterproductive. In my waiting room, a mother asked her fourteen-year-old son several times to turn down the volume on his portable CD player. He smashed it to the ground and yelled, "There, are you happy now? You broke my radio!" Remember, angry children don't excel at reasoning, and they believe that if they are angry, they must be right. It's an "I may not win, but at least you won't either" attitude.

Angry children also attack to manipulate. A twelve-year-old described locking his mother in a room when she refused to allow him to see a late movie with friends. He wanted both to punish her, as he felt he was being punished, and he also hoped to weaken her resolve so she would let him go to the movie in the end.

Nor are all their efforts this direct. Other kids move into a pattern of organized meanness. These children spread lies about their family members, friends, or teachers. For example, kids today are savvy enough to know that if they accuse a teacher of making a racial slur or touching them inappropriately, the matter will be dealt with immediately, even if the allegations are completely false. Spreading rumors about others can sometimes have a more brutal effect than a direct attack.

Angry children may use attacks against themselves as another form of aggression. This happens when you hear, "I hate myself" or "I can't do anything right." Attacks can be as subtle as a girl who dresses in sloppy, dirty clothes reasoning, "No one likes me anyway. This is what I deserve." Ignoring homework or quitting a sports team may also be signs of pain that call for a parent's concern. These actions are red flags. Something major may be bothering the child that requires immediate action or even professional help to uncover the problem that prompted these self-attacks.

How to help

With a limited repertoire of responses, children need to learn new techniques. These might include: a personal time-out; a brainstorm session of alternative reactions; or role-playing another way of handling the problem. One father, tired of his children fighting over who watched what TV program, sent them off to come up with a list of five ideas for solving the problem, and said the TV wasn't going back on until they had a workable list of alternatives. Off they went to another room. At first they came up with only more bickering and went their separate ways in disgust. The older son refused to work on it the next day as a way to annoy his siblings even further. By the third day, however, they all missed their favorite TV shows so much that they were finally motivated to sit down and work it out.

If approached correctly, children welcome new ways of problem-solving, for these ultimately give them the power and control over the situation at hand that they so crave. No child relishes feeling overwhelmed by anger and frustration. Constructive conflict-solving offers the angry child clear, long-term rewards. Empowering a child with other methods to confront problems more effectively can have a remarkable effect on quieting her impulse to attack. (See Chapter 7 for more on conflict-solving techniques.)

7. ANGRY CHILDREN USE ANGER TO GAIN POWER

Some parents feel that their child runs the house. These angry children use their anger to control their world and manipulate others.

I remember six-year-old Domenic, who lived alone with his mom. His parents were going through a divorce as tumultuous as their marriage had been. Domenic witnessed his father's drinking and saw him hit his mother on several occasions. The anger lived on in young Domenic, who would yell at his mom whenever he didn't get his way. He ordered her about and even punched her in fits of rage.

Domenic explained to me that he was angry at his mom for not protecting herself from his dad. His mom retreated from her husband, so Domenic felt he had to take over. Tragically, his dad's behavior was Domenic's role model. One time, his parents got into an argument when his father picked up his mail from the house. After he left, Domenic yelled, "You make Daddy stop or I'm going to beat you up!"

Children who grow up in a world where anger is a source of power and influence learn to use this angry power over family and peers to control an out-of-control family situation. It also compensates for the powerlessness children feel using calmer solutions for day-to-day problems. Each child learns that anger gets them what they want—a toy, a favor, relaxing of the rules, or just keeping others at a distance.

Bullies are born of this desire for control. Bullies learn that acting tough has a powerful payoff. In some circles, they gain social status, as other kids do their bidding out of fear. When the bully is a member of a group of tough kids, there's an even greater sense of power. The bully can intimidate parents, teachers, and other children into getting what he wants just with a look. One sixteen-year-old who habitually dressed in a long leather coat and heavy boots referred to this getup as his "power clothes." "Even strangers know to back off when they see me coming," he explained. "I don't have to say a word and I get what I want."

It's not only the street fighter or gun-toting gang member that uses anger to intimidate. An All-American facade can hide an angry master manipulator. It can be the quiet loner who intimidates others by acting weird. It can be the lonely computer whiz who sends a virus to paralyze the school computer. The bully can be a girl who uses gossip to hurt her classmates. It can be the outwardly happy child who anonymously vandalizes school property with graffiti.

The manipulative side shows up whenever and wherever the child feels the need. Many angry children show their bullying personality only at home. She may be a tantrum-throwing terror with Mom and Dad, but a delight at Grandma's. Another child can hide his sister's books the night before an exam, but appear studious and respectful at school.

Words (or refusal to use them) are often the power tools for angry kids. They may use words to get others in trouble. When you ask questions, they may know the answer but respond with a shrug and an "I don't know" to be in control of the negative information.

Criticism, belittling, gossip, and sarcasm are other verbal tools of control. Criticism is a way of finding fault in others' successes, aimed at taking away any respect that would come to them. Angry kids learn to manipulate arguments by setting traps to get parents more angry, to change the subject, or to confuse the issues. The varied verbal techniques kids use in arguments are such major power tools that I address them in more detail in Chapter 7.

Threats and physical force are the other common tools of control. Provoking a fight gives children from toddlers to teens a sense of power. Angry kids are constantly vigilant of this. Fights and threats test out that power.

Children who fight the house rules attempt to control discipline by undermining it. The parents of a five-year-old complained, "We spank him and he laughs at us, saying 'It doesn't hurt.' We put him in his room and he rips the sheets off the bed and throws clothes around. We give him a time-out and he jumps on the chair." That boy feels he is getting control back in this battle of wits even though there are clearly no winners here.

How to help

These manipulative children try to undermine adult authority to avoid discipline. Yet I've never met an angry child who really wants to live with all this anger. They want peace. They want parents to provide a safe and loving household. But if they live in a world filled with pain or stress, in which they don't trust adults to help them fix their problems, they will not give up their power without a fight. When a parent lays down the law, the angry child will put parents to the test to see who is *really* in control.

Even if you pass the test once or twice, it doesn't mean you're off the hook. Angry kids continue to set traps to see if you're strong or clever enough to maintain control.

It's as if kids are saying, "Unless you prove you're more powerful, then I'll be in control. If you try to take control, I'll test your strength. If I win, you're not strong and don't deserve to rule." Statements like, "You can't make me do anything" or "I don't have to listen to you," are challenges. But if you win, you may find the resistance turns into respect.

Getting help from professionals

Angry kids also hold on to control when parents try to get professional help for them. I have known many a family who called me, desperate to make an appointment, only to cancel because their child refused to come. Others may go to their appointment but not cooperate.

"I said I'd come here," said a seventeen-year-old girl, "but I never said I would talk." So she sat silently in the waiting room while her mother and I talked. These kids hold their families hostage, digging in their heels and proclaiming they don't need help. If the parent once again gives in, the power goes right back to the child. As long as they feel in control, they are reluctant to change. They are more likely to let go when they learn to trust their ability to solve problems by other means.

Counseling is not designed to put anyone "back in their place." The goal in counseling families with angry children focuses on putting the family back in balance. The child may have taken control because parents have given up their authority. This creates a power vacuum that the angry child all too willingly fills. Counseling focuses on helping parents be parents and kids be kids. It builds mutual respect by replacing fear and intimidation with proper parenting and communication.

In addition to using counseling to untangle the control issues, parents can help their child by using discipline effectively and consistently. They can also listen to children's concerns in order to teach the value of communication in solving problems.

8. ANGRY CHILDREN INDULGE IN DESTRUCTIVE SELF-TALK

Angry children build and maintain anger by carrying on arguments long before a conversation begins and forever after it ends. Angry children start arguments within their own minds and rehearse aggressive ways of handling problems. They spin each scenario out to its worst conclusion, imagining bad situations and seeking preemptive retaliation. This makes their reactions even more intense. Think for a minute of yourself, perhaps upset about something at work, then driving home and snapping at the first person you see. This angry self-talk keeps the anger going far beyond reasonable limits.

No one else has to say or do anything. Kids carry on conversations in their minds that make them ready to bite off someone's head just for breathing, let alone talking.

When Nick told his mother about a bad day at school, he was upset by what seemed to him unfair censure from his teacher.

"She always catches me and never picks on anyone else," he said.

His mother suggested he might have avoided the trouble if he hadn't spoken out in class. Nick went to his room but came back in a few minutes, even angrier.

"I've been thinking about what you said, but you're wrong. My teacher *does* have it out for me. Even if I was quiet she'd find something to criticize me for. She's a witch." Stunned by this strong reaction, his mother sent him back to his room to cool off. Instead he did just the opposite, working himself into a lather. When he emerged half an hour later, his face was red and he seemed to have been engaged in a shouting match with his absent teacher.

"I hate her," he roared. "I don't care what you say. I hate her! And tomorrow I'm going to get back at her."

How to help

Parents can help by teaching the child how rehearsing negative thoughts keeps them angry. Instead of sending him to his room to cool off, Nick's mom would have done better to talk with him and help him better understand the problem. Rehearsing positive thoughts could have calmed him and worked toward building solutions.

Realize that everybody talks to himself. It's like having a sports commentator giving a play-by-play description in our heads. Self-talk can get us worried or calm us. Angry self-talk magnifies molehills into mountains and small problems into rage. The next time your child overreacts to something you say, assume that he began the argument hours before you even entered the room.

Helping the angry child often involves replacing the angry self-defeating script in her head with other, more productive dialogues. Psychologists refer to this as "thought stopping." When she begins to ruminate over an injustice or anticipate a confrontation, teach her to rehearse a happy ending rather than a negative one. Work with your child to identify angry self-talk and practice stopping the thought in its tracks, and rehearsing plans to solve the problem.

9. ANGRY CHILDREN CONFUSE ANGER WITH SELF-ESTEEM

Angry children suffer from self-esteem problems that feed their anger. Though angry children tend to confuse all bad feelings with anger, lack of self-esteem is particularly insidious because it can undermine the child's well-being in so many areas of her life. For instance, a child with poor self-esteem may feel unliked by her peers and experience such profound loneliness that she lashes out in anger. However, it's not always apparent that a child lacks self-esteem. Some carry with them an air of bravado and arrogance that makes them appear self-assured when they are not.

How can a gregarious child be friendless or a talented child lack confidence? How can a child who is constantly praised think so little of himself? Why would a child continue to pick fights when it only causes more misery for himself? These speak to the complexity of self-esteem where a child's level of confidence seems to belie their experiences.

One would think that a child struggling with poor self-esteem would jump at the chance to win back affection. Instead these kids tend to hold back or even make their situations worse. For example, a parent may try to help a child with poor self-esteem by offering compliments. The child may lash back with, "Like I really care what you think of me."

Self-esteem is an essential component of healthy psychological development. Without it, a talented child may fail. With it, a child can work to transform average skills into success. In order to understand the angry child, we must understand the components of their self-esteem and how it got so confused.

Some psychologists have defined self-esteem simply as feeling good about yourself. When we equate self-esteem with feeling good, however, we can fall into the trap of raising our children to focus on immediate gratification while avoiding the difficult path toward long-term goals. Healthy self-esteem, however, comes from our ability to successfully handle life's difficulties while respecting others. Thus, self-esteem is best viewed in the context of the family and society, not just as the fulfillment of personal desires.

The importance of fostering good self-esteem puts a great deal of pressure on parents who want to encourage their children. Is there such a thing as too much praise? Should you praise the child or praise the behavior? Is it wrong to compliment a child who gave only a half-hearted effort? And if you don't do any of these things exactly right, is your child doomed to a life of failure?

Parents should take heart in the fact that self-esteem is not so easily built or eroded. It takes more than praise to build confidence and more than a slip of the parent's lip to tear it down. Self-esteem grows from many experiences, and even mistakes are sources of learning, not shame.

Self-esteem has four components—value, resilience, focus, and integrity. How a child rates on each of these four components will determine the quality of his or her self-esteem.

Value: Value is a function of our personal assessment of our talents and of ourselves as people. A child rates her own ability to draw, run, sing, or do schoolwork in comparison to others and her own goals, and values herself accordingly.

But a child may also feel positive or negative about who he *is,* not just what he can *do.* Global self-judgments such as "I am a good person" or "What I do is worthwhile" may contribute more to strong self-esteem than any single skill such as the ability to run fast or excel at math. Likewise, the child can have a poor sense of himself if he feels "I'm not worth having as a friend" or "I can't do anything right."

There is a strong, instinctive desire to feel self-worth. We all want to feel important, so we seek activities, friends, and experiences that shore up our positive feelings. When a child feels negative about who she is, she'll avoid people and experiences that could remind her of failures. Who wants to be around other kids who are constant

Integrity: The fourth component of self-esteem is the ability to deal honestly with oneself and others. The honest child has the benefit of objectivity, stepping back and assessing without distortion. This child can admit her faults and learn from them. She'll also benefit from advice and constructive criticism.

The dishonest child lies to himself, remaining in his own eyes the poor victim of another's action even when he was clearly at fault. He'll say with conviction his mom never told him he had to clean his room before he could go to the party.

Children lacking integrity will lie to impress friends. Jeremy told his classmates that he won a contest entitling him and friends to front-row hockey playoff seats. The prize included dinner with a player and a limousine ride. His peers spent the next three weeks tripping over each other with acts of kindness toward Jeremy. When they discovered the contest never existed, Jeremy spent days defending himself in playground fights. He also blamed them for being stupid enough to believe the contest ever existed. His own brittle self-esteem didn't give him the confidence to deal straightforwardly with his friends, so he tried to create an aura of success that other children would admire. In doing so, he was dishonest with them and with himself.

Dishonesty also preserves the self to avoid guilt. A child with good self-esteem can admit his failures and wrongdoings even if it's painful. The angry child avoids this pain by rewriting history to cast himself as the hero or the victim, not the perpetrator.

How to help

You can help the angry child in a number of ways. First, give honest but not phony or overblown praise. Kids develop self-esteem when given challenges a bit above their ability. Being too protective and avoiding challenges has the opposite effect, as does encouraging them to achieve a goal far beyond their reach. Expose your child to a wide range of activities. The more he experiences, the better sense he gets of where his talents and interests may lie. Let your child have a say in what he tries. You don't have to let him choose every activity, but as the years go by, he'll give you a good idea of what he can and can't do. Make sure he follows through on commitments. Also, understand that tastes change. Phoebe may be willing to play piano for three years, but after a while it may be time to hang it up.

Never agree to unhealthy goals. This might include the angry child who wants to own a gun, letting underage kids drink alcohol at home so they won't drink it elsewhere, giving the bully boxing lessons, buying the intimidating clothes and violent music or video games.

Participate in activities with your child. Practice baseball, attend performances, show an interest in their interests. And remember that building self-confidence means sometimes you have to let go. When he is ready—teach him, if he needs help—give help, but let him do it for himself when he can.

10. ANGRY CHILDREN CAN BE NICE WHEN THEY WANT TO BE

Frequently, an angry child will choose one or several persons as angry targets. They may be wonderful with teachers while wretched with parents. Some are more openly angry with a permissive parent because they can get away with it without losing their affection permanently.

Even an angry child is able to show genuine affection. Her kindness may be shown to particular groups, perhaps at school, but not at home. They may display it at certain times not just to manipulate, but because the love is genuine.

For instance, a child who might otherwise be complaining and bullying might become a saint overnight if his mom catches the flu. He'll fluff pillows, talk with her, even offer to make chicken soup. But once Mom gets back on her feet, the courtesies stop. Why? Perhaps when Mom was sick he felt worried and vulnerable. Perhaps he felt the genuine concern that speaks to his love for her. Perhaps the nurturing is a positive tool he had learned from his family. Or perhaps he knows that when Mom is sick, there is no need to threaten since she is unable to exercise control over him.

Parents of angry children frequently describe them as a mixture of saint and sinner. They really can be warm and affectionate. At such moments parents realize these are not bad kids. But the sweet child they know is in there may come and go, according to the child's immediate needs.

It's critical that parents learn to recognize when their child's pleasant behavior is authentic, and when it's a means to manipulation. A child might refuse to clean his room and end up in a screaming match with his parent. The result: being grounded for a week, even if it means he misses a ball game he's scheduled to play in, and losing the power struggle.

But what if the child grounded on Monday cleans up on Wednesday, butters up Mom and Dad on Thursday, and then on Friday is rewarded by getting to go to his game? What happens is, the child has taken control again.

When a child's acts of kindness come only in an attempt to win favors or stop a punishment, parents should steel themselves to stand firm. As long as the discipline you've meted out is fair, there's little reason to change it. When angry children find their manipulation pays off, it only reinforces their anger at being punished in the first place. Avoid the temptation to reward the manipulation. He may protest and say "you should let me off being grounded because I was good today." You can remind him that being good is exactly what you expect of him all the time, not just when he wants a reward.

By the same token, though, a spontaneous expression of love or thoughtfulness should be taken at face value and embraced.

There are three steps to helping the angry child who is conveniently kind. First, know the rules and stick with them. Second, where problems exist with a specific person, find out why and work on it. Third, nurture the genuine caring as a strength to use in other relationships.

Please note after reading this chapter that if you've identified a few of these traits in your own child, daily practice of the strategies in this book may indeed help calm your child and your home. If, on the other hand, your child has many of these characteristics, counseling with a trained professional may be the more prudent course. When in doubt, take your child for an evaluation.

Chapter Four

Home-Grown Anger

THE FAMILY is the single most important influence in a child's psychological development.
For better or worse, our families influence us in ways
that we carry throughout our life. Let's face it, there
are no perfect families. Each has its share of tough
times, and the ability to weather such difficulties is
one of the greatest strengths of a well-functioning
family. A good family isn't necessarily one that never
has arguments, money problems, or illness. A good
family, rather, is one that rallies around each member to help him or her through life's problems.

Members of strong families support each other
through the changes that come from growth and
development and through tough times. They embrace one another's different personalities while ap-
preciating the strength of the family unit. They also
work together when problems arise, and they tend to
have pleasant relationships with the extended family
and are involved with others in the community.
Healthy families have a good sense of humor. And

when problems brew, they attack the problems—not each other. Their greatest strength is their motivation to work together toward healing.

Some families are filled with pain, stress, power games, or indulgence, which sabotages their own health—even families that may look "ideal" to the casual observer. In this chapter we'll look at the four types of families that tend to produce the angry child, as well as the less supportive environments where children can become unhappy without anyone even noticing it.

I realize that it may be uncomfortable to read, let alone admit, that your family may be reinforcing—or even causing—your child's anger. But discovering the roots of your child's problem can be very empowering. Many families I've worked with would rather hear that their child was angry because of the ills of society or a chemical imbalance so the family would not have to feel any blame. But as I've pointed out to them, in such cases, the parents would be powerless to help their child. So while it's tough to admit that your family's style, habits, or interactions have contributed to creating an angry child, the good news is: If you are part of the problem, you have the power to be part of the solution.

If your child's anger results solely from a medical condition, you might only be able to manage the symptoms. With familial roots, you cannot only reach out to the angry child, but prevent her siblings from following the same angry path, and restore much peace and hope to your home.

Keep in mind as you read through this chapter that two or more of these patterns are present in many families. Rather than assign your family a label, look for patterns that may describe your home life, and then look for ways you can overcome these unhealthy patterns. Don't get caught up in denial or self-recrimination; that's not the point. Family influences *can* be altered and improved dramatically, and the results—having a happy, pleasant child who is comfortable with himself and others—is certainly worth the effort and self-examination.

How Parenting Styles Affect Anger

Just as parenting styles can bring out the best in a child, other styles can accent the worst. This is very difficult to read, I'm sure. No wonder. Parents are often overcome by fear and guilt when they realize they may have had a little or a lot to do with their child's anger. Our own behavior as parents—namely how we love, reward, and discipline our children, and how available we are—invariably influences a child's personality.

When our child's temperament and our parenting style match, there are good feelings on the home front. When communication is poor and sensibilities diverge, parents may not know instinctively how to deal effectively with their child. Our mistakes add up. For the most part, kids bounce back, and parents often learn through hindsight, but when problems persist, the child's anger can build.

Granted, it's hard to know what a child needs. Different kids react differently to the same parents. The child's personal experiences, basic temperament, genetic inheritance, and developmental stages all play roles. Keep in mind too that you may be treating your own children differently, especially if they are of different genders. It's a subtle dance that requires constant reevaluation and recalibrating based on who and where your child is at any given point in his development.

But over the years that I've worked with angry children and observed them with their parents, I've learned that anger bespeaks a variety of conditions that can be traced to four home environments:

- **In the Troubled Family,** anger is the voice of pain
- **In the Frantic Family,** anger is the voice of stress
- **In the Angry Family,** anger is the voice of power
- **In the Indulging Family,** anger is the voice of desire

Let's look at each of these four in turn.

The Troubled Family

The troubled family is overwhelmed by hurt. They may be dealing with divorce, financial woes, drug or alcohol abuse, mental illness, or death of a family member. Note, I don't include issues of potential abuse here, as that's covered later in the angry family.

Kids in troubled families lash out against and try to relieve the pain that has infected their home life. Their anger can be a barometer, signaling that this pain is not being addressed, and that it demands attention.

GRIEVING FAMILIES

All families are struck by tragedy at one time or another, but when a troubled family loses a close family member, they may be so caught up in grieving that they're emotionally unavailable to each other. The same factors exist when a prolonged illness overwhelms the family's ability to cope. The pain is multiplied for a child who finds it unacceptable to show his feelings.

When Warren was ten years old, his sister lost her lengthy battle with leukemia, and died. Now fifteen, Warren had only recently begun intense fighting with his parents when they came to see me. His parents hoped counseling would heal Warren, who had never seemed to grieve his sister's loss. I soon realized Warren's inability to deal with his emotions wasn't focused on his sister as much as upon his parents. In Warren's eyes, they'd spent significant time mourning for the girl, talking about her, and doing things for her long after she died. When Warren needed them, they weren't there, and he felt any emotion on his part would have appeared insignificant in comparison to the magnitude of their grief. After all, he was still alive. So he kept his feelings to himself until they could no longer be contained and then he'd blow up over minor difficulties. When his parents responded with punishment, it only drove Warren farther away.

More than anything I could provide, Warren needed his family. It sounds simple, but not when you consider what the family was going through at the time. Warren's whole life turned around when his parents were finally able to let go of her and embrace him.

Some families build emotional walls to prevent feeling pain ever again. The trouble is, such walls also prevent them from forming much needed attachments. And in some families, the members blame one another, as if to say, "You weren't strong enough to protect my sister so how can I know you'll take care of me?" These issues can weigh a family down; unless they deal with them openly, the pain continues.

Families who have suffered the loss of a loved one would do well to investigate grief counseling, which is available in most parts of the country. Even a trip to the bookstore can be healing. In her book *What's Heaven?*, Maria Shriver helps to explain the death of a loved one to young children, who do ask thought-provoking and sometimes very startling questions about death. Other good resources are *Help Me Say Goodbye: Activities for Helping Kids Cope When a Special Person Dies,* by Janis Silverman; and *Healing the Grieving Child's Heart: 100 Practical Ideas for Families, Friends & Caregivers,* by Alan D. Wolfelt, Ph.D.

ADDICTED FAMILIES

Another source of anger for children is an addiction in their family. Life with an addicted parent is difficult at best, but often the whole family gets so caught up in the addictive patterns that they unknowingly contribute to the very addiction causing so much pain.

Alcohol, drugs, gambling, or other dependencies all contribute to an ailing family psyche. Most addicts' efforts to break their dependencies keep their families emotionally on the hook through their ups and downs.

Although many addicts deny their behavior has any influence on the family, it's important to realize that they often deny an addiction exists in the first place. Denial is a fundamental characteristic of addiction. It gets in the way of much needed help, for the addict or the child's reactions.

Addictions consume money, emotional energy, and communication. The addict's major goal becomes handling that addiction. He or she may still go to work, bring home a paycheck, and even show a good deal of love and concern for others. But if a child's needs stand between a parent and the addiction, it's a different story.

The child who knows a parent is drunk, doped up, or frantic over a lost bet, at least knows what he is dealing with. But when the parent is trying to hide the real cause, the child doesn't know if it's her fault. She just knows something isn't right. She may try harder and harder to please her dad, hoping he will show her more attention. What she does not realize is that she is on the losing end of a competition with the addiction.

Even families that have acknowledged the addiction in their midst are often ashamed and don't seek help, passing the cycle of denial on to the next generation. People in the addicted family don't learn how to solve problems, they learn how to survive. Many kids experience pain they simply aren't equipped to handle. When that pain turns to anger, they may lash out at the addict or even at the nonaddicted parent, blaming them for the situation with phrases like, "If you treated Daddy better he wouldn't have to drink." Moreover, anger may not remain inside the confines of the home.

MENTAL ILLNESS IN FAMILIES

When a family member suffers from mental illness or depression, children find themselves struggling to understand the parent's behaviors and emotions. Just as with the addict, the depressed parent is hardly available to share joy in a child's accomplishments. That parent may wrestle not only with emotions, but with tremendous guilt and shame for failing to parent actively enough.

Sixteen-year-old Kristi told me how her manic-depressive mom would frantically clean the house, read, talk endlessly, and joke around with little sleep for days, only to plummet into a morbid suicidal state. It left her worried that whenever her mom seemed happy, gloom would soon follow.

Caught up on this emotional roller coaster, Kristi felt she couldn't survive. She spent much of her time worrying about her mother, and her grades suffered. This led to fights about homework and school that eventually she used as a teenage excuse to get out among her friends. Fortunately, many mental illnesses respond to medication and can restore the individual to a more hopeful existence. When a family member has a significant mental illness, a network of professionals who can work with them toward solutions is critical.

MARITAL DISCORD IN FAMILIES

One of the most common sources of pain for children is living through their parents' marital problems. The issues of divorce and custody battles loom so large that I've devoted a later chapter to it, but even in marriages that don't come apart, observing their parents' struggles is overwhelming for most kids. A child may lash out in anger at both parents—the one she's closest to (because that parent is safe) or the one she feels is "at fault." Whatever the dynamics, one must recognize that the child's anger is symptomatic of the troubled marriage, not justification for either parent that the other is bad.

SOLUTIONS FOR TROUBLED FAMILIES

What can you do about the angry child in the troubled family? As I've said earlier, anger is usually associated with another negative emotion, and if one hopes to stop the anger, the real focus has to be on stopping the trigger emotion. Ongoing counseling can help the family understand its problem, learn to work together, and set a course to a better way of problem-solving techniques. One issue the family will eventually come to terms with is forgiveness. When children live with pain and hurt, they may carry that burden with them for life and torment themselves with questions such as "Why couldn't my family have been better?" or "Why is this so unfair?"

It's very tough to heal the pain, but blame keeps that pain alive. Other family members and friends can help teach a child to forgive. This doesn't mean minimizing the problems and suffering, nor does it mean you go on as if nothing happened. It *does* mean helping the child relinquish his desire to get even, that you stop seeking revenge. All of this may have to take place in the absence of an apology from the very person who caused the child so much misery. This is a great injustice in troubled families. In fact, the process may take years, but the alternative is to store up so much anger and hatred that the child becomes the very person she resented. Forgiveness allows children to move forward, to direct energy back toward healing and understanding, and to move on with their lives.

Several characteristics of angry children—poor analysis and problem-solving, manipulation and control, and confused self-esteem—are especially prevalent in troubled families. Review these traits for help with these children and take solace in the knowledge that some kids in troubled families end up remarkably well adjusted, learning to handle life despite the problems that actually strengthen them and teach them to grow.

The Frantic Family

"Imagine this schedule," said a mother of three I once counseled. "Each week I have to deal with soccer practices and games, dance rehearsal, piano lessons, tutoring, and homework. Each day is filled to the brim, and I feel like I spend most of it in the car, driving, eating on the fast-food circuit, and stopping arguments in the car or over the cell phone. You'd think that with all I do for them, they would show more gratitude and less attitude."

Meet the frantic family—overscheduled, overwhelmed, and under enormous stress. It's not that the parents don't care; in fact, some would say they care too much, as they get their children involved in everything the community offers. Unfortunately, we forget kids also need time to learn how to take care of themselves, and they can't do that if they have every minute scheduled. It's as if parents are so afraid of allowing kids to entertain themselves that they give them every gadget, toy, TV, or video game to ward off boredom. Families need time to relax, have fun, be creative, and just enjoy one another's company.

Sometimes we fall into a frantic mode unintentionally. I don't know anyone who would rather spend hours slaving over work they brought home in the briefcase than with the child who needs attention or wants to have fun with her parent. But when we're trying to do too much, whether it's work-related, caring for sick relatives, or home projects, the modus operandi becomes less action and more reaction. And when the adults are overwhelmed, the tension filters down to the children. Between their unrealistic schedule for the children and the lack of quiet family time, frantic families often feel they must scream to be heard. So for the angry child in the frantic family, anger is the voice of stress.

Why are they angry when their parents have worked so hard at making them feel good? Because frantic families (a) don't pay attention to developmental needs of their children, and (b) they deny their own part in the frenzy (especially if they are overcommitted themselves). Frantic families don't talk through problems except at the traffic light; they're too darned busy. When they do face problems, they seek the microwave solution because all others require more work and the commitment of time they don't feel they can make. And frantic families maintain such a high level of tension that tempers easily snap.

One mother of a volatile seventeen-year-old had daily fights with her son over unfinished homework. When, he'd shout, did she expect him to finish it? One look at his schedule showed he had no time after school with football and soccer practice followed by tutoring. He didn't even get home until eight o'clock every night, and by then he was exhausted. Always juggling two or three things concurrently, he never spent time in concentrated study.

Even when some parents cut back on the scheduling, frantic kids don't know how to sit down and engage in prolonged study. They only know last-minute cramming. While the frantic family might qualify as excellent circus jugglers, they are just plain lousy at setting the right priorities.

Kids like this get so used to schedule overload that they go through withdrawal on a quiet evening at home, becoming restless and agitated, complaining there's nothing to do. Reminding them that the extra time would be just right for studying can result in a fight because they've become accustomed to glancing at the books moments before a test or firing off a vague version of homework. These study methods rarely yield good results, and in fact perpetuate a cycle of feeling lousy about the situation, and about oneself. Who wouldn't be angry?

Many frantic families might benefit from counseling, but here's what I've found: Someone will call to schedule an urgent appointment, only to cancel later with an excuse ranging from "We forgot" or "Something came up." Even worse is when a parent tells me, "Mary is doing much better today and she had a great day yesterday, so I think we can hold off another week." This problem gets back-burnered until the child explodes. They wait until the level of the child's anger rises above the stress level of the frantic family.

Take another family I worked with. This single-parent family with children aged nine, twelve, and fourteen, attended three different practices for each (soccer, ballet, and baseball) in three different parts of town, at least three to five days each week. Two kids took piano lessons and another art lessons. The fourteen-year-old baby-sat three times a week, and each child required almost two hours of homework or study time nightly. Inevitably, their teachers saw that their homework was slipping, as well as their test scores. So how do you think the mother answered this?

"I think I better talk to the teacher about giving them less homework," she told me.

This was not exactly the solution I was looking for, but it hardly surprised me either. It goes back to setting the right priorities. Is the major task of childhood to run around or to succeed in school? Many kids cannot handle the schedules inflicted upon them. In the case of one family, I did get the mother to limit the after-school activities to one per child, and this helped them find the necessary time for studies. Of course, Mom had to give up her "keep up with the Joneses" idea, once she made her peace with having less than superstar kids. She too was less stressed, and the family prospered as a result.

I once formed a counseling group for parents of frantic families. Their beeping pagers and ringing cell phones frequently interrupted the first session. We were all able to laugh at these ringing examples of how hectic their lives had become. A rule that all pagers and phones were to be turned off allowed us to concentrate on the family issues. Ironically, these parents said they looked forward to our sessions as the only peace they had.

The family with some quiet time actually has the opportunity to solve problems. Frantic families say "We'll talk about it later," but that moment never arrives. As a therapist, it seemed to me that the time these families spent talking in my office was the only time they talked together all week. When frantic families have no time to work through things, problems build. Workable, little problems get ignored, and only crises get attention. Kids learn to make even small matters into federal crises in order to wrench their distracted parents' focus onto them.

Frantic families may genuinely want advice to reduce anger, but they're often not willing to make the necessary changes. An eight-year-old who had his family in knots loved the attention he received each week in my office. But even then the family wasn't able to set aside their outside concerns and give their child their full interest—with Mom glancing at her watch and brother complaining he was late for his game. Not until I worked around their schedules, finding a time in which everyone could engage fully, did they make enough progress and become able to make changes in their life.

SOLUTIONS FOR THE FRANTIC FAMILY

If the level of stress in your home has reached an intolerable point due to overscheduling, lack of time for quiet interaction, and there is an overriding aura of crisis, here are a few strategies:

- First, slow down. Sounds easy, but a hectic pace is hard to give up.
- Make family time a top priority. Put it on the calendar, and demand that everyone be home together. Children will follow the parents' lead here. Sharing mealtimes and doing something fun together after weekend worship are good examples.
- Turn down the noise. In the car, when moving between activities, or at home, use the time to communicate and listen to each other. Turn off the radio or TV during quiet times to reduce stimulation. Outlaw TV, telephone, stereo, or reading during meals. Insist everyone remain seated so that everyone is heard.
- If you have a car phone, get off of it. Talk with your kids in the car rather than all your friends. Teach calming exercises such as thinking soothing thoughts and listening to quiet music.
- Reduce the number of activities your children participate in. I've never met a child whose emotional problem resulted from *not* being allowed to partake in multiple after-school activities, but the converse is definitely not true. Ask her to pick one activity, and don't be surprised if she has a tough time prioritizing. This is symptomatic of individuals in a frantic family. Rest assured, however, that you aren't punishing a child by requiring him to read a book or find something else to occupy his time that doesn't involve a scheduling commitment and many dollars' worth of equipment.
- Bring problems, even the small ones, to family meetings. Be alert to the signs of troubles brewing, and address them sooner rather than letting them fester and erupt later. (See Chapter 7 for suggestions on how to run effective family meetings.)

The Angry Family

Angry families are those in which the adults themselves are angry, short-tempered, or critical people. They may be emotionally abusive, resorting to name-calling or nasty threats. They may use their physical advantage to control, intimidate, or smash cherished objects in a fit of rage. They may even threaten violence. When you witness an angry family member literally "lose it," you never know for certain if you're next. Anger is sometimes meted out silently by refusing to communicate, or by setting up situations that inevitably result in another's actions that carry the basis of an argument later.

The angry parent models the power of anger. This person never learned to control anger and handles children with screams and threats like "Do it now, or you'll be sorry!" These parents end up enforcing emotions rather than rules. When angry, they take action. When calm, they let problems slide. Children learn to read their parents' moods to stay out of trouble, but they also learn from their model of the angry behavior. Some children react to this by becoming meek and withdrawn, but others see the world through an angry parent's negative eyes, and in turn use anger to control others as well.

Parents play a major role in teaching their children how to handle life's difficulties. If the parent approaches her own problems calmly, the child will learn to be thoughtful. But if the child sees the parent losing his temper whenever challenges arise, then the child learns to react impulsively and with blasts of anger that blow the problems away rather than solve them.

Hot-tempered adults may have Jekyll-and-Hyde-like mood swings. They can be kind and loving, but they also have a nasty streak that emerges all too often. These parents may be the ones who react with road rage toward the driver that passed them in traffic, or belittled the sales clerk who couldn't answer a question. They can be the coworker you tiptoe around.

So what do such parents teach their children? They show that anger gets attention and action. When a child sees an angry mother get kid-glove care at the store, or an angry father intimidate his wife into submissiveness, they learn firsthand that anger is the voice of power and gets results. It won't be long before the child tries these behaviors on for size himself.

Angry children may not show their anger to the powerful parent. After all, they don't want to battle an angry parent. They'll find someone else to intimidate. The anger may erupt in other places, like school, or the child may focus his anger on the object of his angry parent's ire, bullying his other parent or sibling.

Sixteen-year-old Jason, for instance, grew up in a home where his father was constantly ridiculing and threatening his mother. Not only did Jason learn he could do the same to her, but he found his father supported him in his actions, as if to emphasize his power over his wife.

Around angry parents, children also learn to read moods, not rules. In an angry household it's a far more valuable survival skill to know what kind of mood Mom is in than to know the rules. Angry parents bark orders each day that are different from the day before, whether to vent or to intimidate. Later, when the parent is calm, the very thing that led to a huge fight the day before may be ignored.

"When I grew up," said Tammy, now twenty-five, "we'd often ask each other what kind of mood Dad was in. If he was in a good mood, we could get away with anything, but if he was in a bad mood, we couldn't do anything right."

An angry parent can skew the dynamics of the entire household. When the other parent tries to buffer the angry adult's mood swings by giving in or becoming the doormat, it reinforces the child's view that might makes right.

Since the angry parent yells, screams, threatens, hits, or uses other tactics of intimidation to get his way, it's understandable that a child equates anger with power. It doesn't matter who is right or wrong, or if the rule exists or not. What matters is whether you have the power to influence events and make your voice heard above all others.

In such a household, communication suffers. The child becomes less concerned with honesty or trying to communicate and is more concerned with keeping the angry adult calm. But once a child has learned that anger can be a power source, this knowledge may infect their action like a disease. Soon, they model the angry parent's behavior with teachers and other adults. Kids learn to belittle. They learn it doesn't matter if you keep your temper. They learn that respect for others is only measured in terms of how much you can intimidate them. When you don't get your way, then you should yell, and people will back off.

This doesn't mean angry parents condone such behavior in their kids. Yet even if the parent tries to get the angry child to stop, the child may protest, saying, "If it's okay for you, then it's okay for me." As James Baldwin reminded us, "Children have never been very good at listening to their elders, but they have never failed to imitate them."

I don't want to paint a totally grim picture of these families, for many can be helped. Ironically, the child's own behavior can be the motivator that leads the family on the road to change.

John and Linda brought their seven-year-old son to my office complaining of his mean attitude. As we sat down together, I noticed their arguments and cutting comments were so continual that I could barely get a word in. By the time I pointed out one of the barbs, they would be on to the next argument. To get them to slow down and pay attention to how they were acting, I videotaped part of a session, then brought them one at a time to view the tape with me. After John watched himself on tape he sat silently for a few moments and then said "Now I see where he gets it from. He acts just like me." John's embarrassment gave him the insight and motivation to change. It had a remarkable effect on the whole family.

There's so much more to the dynamics of the angry parent, it would take a whole book itself. For now we can describe it only briefly and offer perspective that might set the parent on the road to change.

SOLUTIONS FOR ANGRY PARENTS

If any of the foregoing rings true, know that your anger could well be spilling over into your child's worldview and contributing to her violent outbursts. By the same token, there is no more potent agent for change than your own positive behavior. Try changing your own mode of handling conflict or stress. This is major work indeed, but work you *must* do for your child and for yourself, nonetheless.

Change may not be easy, because anger has worked for you for many years or it may be a long-standing habit. But seeing yourself through your child's behavior may be the catalyst you need to start on your own process of transformation. You know the pain your own anger causes in your life. Do you really want to raise your child to experience the same?

What tends to ignite your anger? Is it high stress at work that you bring home and take out on your family? Use relaxation methods to calm down before you get home. Listen to quiet music, not news or angry talk radio while driving home from the office. Is it deeply ingrained ways of handling things that you never unlearned? Work with a counselor or therapist if your anger has its roots in deeper conflicts. But get help to change your patterns before you take it out on your family any longer.

When you do get angry, clean up the loose ends. Remember the importance of the aftermath. Use it as an opportunity to teach your children how to go back over a problem and solve it. That includes apologies, and reparations to those you have hurt. The angry parent and child both can be fooled into thinking that because they have power, they have wisdom. Show your child that wisdom comes from thoughtful action, not impulsive attacks.

Finally, keep working at it. As the impulsive parent, your greatest failing is assuming that just because you tried anger management once and it didn't work, that it will *never* work. Change takes time in children, and even longer in adults.

The Indulging Family

The fourth type of family teaches children that anger can be a mechanism for fulfilling their wishes. This family has trouble saying "no" to their children—especially when they get mad. These children learn to use their anger to manipulate others; and parents, in turn, indulge the child's wishes rather than face the anger. In the indulging family, anger is the voice of desire.

Parents aren't always aware that they're feeding that desire. It can build subtly over the years as the child graduates from whining to tantrums to attacks. Or it can be a sudden discovery, as when the child finds an outburst in the toy store gets him just what he wanted.

Over time, children learn that anger is effective, so who can blame them for using it to get their way? The tragedy comes when a parent gives in without thinking. Children can intimidate their parents into letting them do all sorts of things that the parent would probably say no to if they could think it through rationally. Furthermore, indulged children never develop any tolerance for coping with stress.

For example, would you buy a child a gun if he yells and screams at you to get him one? Would you give the car keys to a child who threatens that you better not tell him what time to come home? Would you cancel a teacher conference after your child told you to stay out of her business if you know what's good for you? Would you buy a child expensive new sneakers if he threatened to have a tantrum in the store if you did not?

From an objective distance the answer to those questions seems obvious—*no!* But the parent of an angry child knows it's not that easy to say no. For example, when I asked one mother if she would buy a toy for her seven-year-old under the threat of a tantrum, she replied, "You've never seen his tantrums. They are nasty, can last for hours and just aren't worth the misery."

When parents do give in, it can take various forms. The most common are: surrender, confusion, and spoiling.

Surrender

The parent who surrenders has literally thrown in the towel. She feels she cannot take it anymore and is so intimidated by her child's wrath that it is the child, not the adult, who runs the household. Such parents feel it's not just a matter of keeping the peace, it's a matter of survival. They become slaves to the child's anger for fear of being threatened and hurt. They give in to the anger with such statements as, "I don't care anymore," "I can't stand the screaming," or "I'll do anything to avoid a blowup."

The indulging/surrendering parent may be disconnected from the child's life, adopting a hands-off attitude toward parenting. Such families have no idea what television programs their children watch, what music they listen to, the sports heroes their kids worship, or the websites they surf. These are families with no knowledge of their teenager's friends or the crowd they hang with. Taken to an extreme, these families may be completely unaware of their child's unsafe or even violent activities: How many times have we wondered how teenagers could amass arsenals without anyone's knowledge in the wake of a school shooting? There are just too many influences that can sneak into your child's life if you aren't observant.

Confusion

The second type of indulging parent is confused about parenting and has shaky skills in that area. They may actually think they're doing the right thing for their children when they give in. Some feel children ought to have all their needs fulfilled, and that leaving *any* wants unfulfilled is somehow unhealthy. These parents may have never sat down and figured out an approach that fits the child's developmental needs. So they may let the mean and obnoxious behavior of the tantrum slide while punishing other misbehaviors, such as neglecting a chore. These are not bad parents. They just don't have a clear and consistent approach when it comes to raising their kids. But when they give in to the threats, tantrums, and meanness, the child still makes the association between losing control and getting her way. Once the child learns that it works, it's hard to get her to stop.

The irony is that parents who send out these confusing messages not only don't discipline their children, but inadvertently reward angry and mean behavior.

Some parents confuse their child's desires with their own adult issues. For instance, they might remember the pain of not having things they wanted as children, or perhaps they feel that giving in to their child will ensure their love.

In some cases parents confuse what's really important in raising a healthy child by using them as pawns in the parent's own battles; such instances are common in divorced households where one spouse indulges their child to reflect badly on the other.

And some parents mistakenly feel that the anger is "just a phase." They believe the angry outbursts and meanness are behaviors their child will grow out of, and they are willing to give in to the tirades "for now." What they don't know is that children don't just "grow out" of things psychologically like they grow out of a pair of shoes. They're helped in that development process by parents who know when to stand firm and when to be nurturing. Often, a child only leaves one developmental stage and moves on to the next because the parent made it worthwhile. For example, a child may need to face the consequences in order to understand why it's better to clean up after himself, to take no for an answer, or to treat people with courtesy.

Spoiling

The third type of indulging parent just plain spoils children. They shower them with gifts, toys, and permissiveness. Children may be let off the hook from taking responsibility for cleaning up after themselves. How many times have you said or thought, "I want it done right, so I'll just do it myself."

Some are caught up in a consumer mentality that convinces them to buy the latest fad their child requests. I remember one mother who felt her son was justified in demanding a third set of $100 athletic shoes even though the two other ones were like new. She reasoned that "all the other kids had them." Other spoiling parents tell themselves, "She is my baby," or "I waited so long to have her, why shouldn't I give her everything," or "I only have visitation once a week, so I want him to feel our time together is special."

Regardless of the reason for giving in to anger (indulging)—whether it's surrender, confusion, or spoiling—the results are the same. The child learns that if he gets angry enough, he gets what he wants. But the angry child faces double jeopardy. The real world isn't a constant series of handouts, which is sometimes a rude awakening for indulged children who expect their demands and desires to be met right away. In never learning to handle their own emotions, they compromise their ability to handle frustration in the future. Rather than learning to earn money and save toward a goal, they'll find ways of manipulating it from adults. One of the characteristics of the angry child is difficulty understanding and empathizing with the feelings of others, and it's easy to see how a child can become that way when he is raised to think only of himself.

SOLUTIONS FOR INDULGING FAMILIES

Recognize that being lenient and overgenerous with your child is not necessarily the best thing for her. If you truly want to give your child everything, think about the intangibles you can bestow that will ultimately help her become a resilient, kind, happy adult by reducing the presence of anger in your home. There are four things indulging parents can do to stop the trend:

■ Get a better understanding of what your child needs. Read books and magazine articles about normal child development and ask for help from experienced parents. Kids need limits. Children without limits at home go out into the world expecting the same, and then when teachers and other adults set rules, the child rebels. Setting limits and teaching children what is acceptable and unacceptable at each age and stage is a very important part of growing. Children need love from a parent, and there should be no limit on that. But they also need to know, at each age, the responsibilities and behaviors expected of them.

■ When you go shopping, have a plan. Bring another adult or relative along to give the child attention, but not stuff! And be ready to stand firm and leave the store if necessary. If you find yourself embarrassed or intimidated by your child's threats and tantrums, you may need a backup plan. Or shop when someone else can watch the children, or order from catalogues or on-line.

■ When it comes to setting limits on household behaviors such as refusals to do chores, find an appropriate and manageable consequence, and set it out clearly. This will be covered further in the chapter on discipline.

■ Build your own supports. Whether it's through a relative, a friend, or a therapist, find someone to whom you can turn for support. This is especially important when you're trying to revise an indulged child's behavior patterns, or when you confuse your own conflicts with your child's needs. If you as a parent have had a tough time setting reasonable limits on your child, it's valuable to have another around as a reality check. You don't have to face this alone. In fact, you're probably better off not facing it solo.

Still Puzzled?

So far we've discovered a lot of influences that contribute to a child's anger. But parents often tell me they just can't figure out what's bugging their child. Lacking any obvious reason to be upset, the child is nonetheless moody, belligerent, or just plain mad at the world. This child's anger puzzles them.

At home, brothers and sisters interact fairly well, and aside from the occasional squabble over coveted toys or borrowed clothes, there doesn't seem to be any friction between siblings. And among the child's friends, he appears to be well-liked and popular, one of the first to be chosen for a team, and invited to every birthday party. There doesn't seem to be a concrete reason for the child's constant outbursts.

Facing this situation, my sense, based upon years in study and in practice, is that just because you don't see a family link to your child's anger doesn't mean it isn't there. And even if the anger is a reflection of trouble adjusting to a phase your child is going through (yes, sometimes it is a phase), or a particular problem he's facing, how you respond to that anger and help him control it will be the most important influence on him. There is always something you can do to quell your child's angry feelings. But it's not always easy to hear.

I might meet with a child and/or his family, and in the first two sessions I've got a pretty good clue what the trouble is and why they've sought counseling. Problem is, it might take me until the sixth, eighth, or tenth session until the parents are ready to hear and accept my findings.

One dad brought his child to see me, and each session, I'd meet with the man briefly. I'd quickly discovered that his son was angry because the family put too much pressure on him, driving him crazy with sports commitments and activities. When the father asked if I knew what was bothering his child, I wasn't sure he could see the problem because he seemed to relish their lifestyle and was a workaholic himself.

I deliberately asked him if he really wanted to know, trying to ease into the findings. He said he did.

So I told him that part of the problem was that his son was overstressed by a hectic schedule without enough family time to simply relax. Sure enough, this man argued that their schedule was just fine. He told me stories of what he had survived growing up. I sensed he wasn't ready to hear that the family's lifestyle was causing his son pain, so I backed off for the time being. But two weeks later the father again asked me, "Dr. Murphy, what do you think the problem is here?"

By now I knew enough about this patient and his family to give a host of examples of how the child's behavior worsened under the stress of too many activities and not enough positive family time. And as I'd said earlier, I felt this man could better accept what I had to say now, than in an earlier visit.

In yet another situation, I met with a mother who was struggling with her three children: two daughters and a son. She too assumed there had to be a missing puzzle piece because these children had everything. Yet the one daughter's grades had started to slide, and while the middle child remained quiet without causing too much worry, the young boy had begun acting out, getting into trouble with teachers.

"Do you mind if I ask you something?" I said, and sensing her acquiescence, I continued. "How's your marriage?"

"Well, what difference does that make? It's the kids we're talking about here!"

Her indignant reaction pretty much confirmed my hunch. She didn't want to admit that her relationship with her husband might be strained, and thereby affecting the household as a unit. This is what I call a denial impasse, and it almost forces the bigger question: "Do you want me to tell you what you want to hear, or what I think you need to know?" It's a very strong and loving parent who can accept the knowledge that their behavior can be at least partly responsible for their child's anger on the spot. Often, it takes time, quiet reflection, or even adult counseling, to confront these issues. But as I've seen time and again, this difficult work is a great gift you can give your child, and it far outweighs the discomfort of facing some of your own demons.

As I've met with thousands of parents through the years, I've been painfully aware that the messages I had to deliver probably sounded harsh. I didn't mean them to be. But I knew that these parents wanted to see their children heal, and to grow out of their troubles with a sense of hope. And the comfort of knowing that the cycle of anger could indeed be broken—and by them—generally came as a huge relief.

It's important to note that the family style is only one of the influences on an angry child. Some children have many factors influencing their behavior, and family is rarely the lone culprit. If the frank examples or descriptions about family influences has been unsettling, the good news is that if the family has had a major negative influence in your child's life—the family at least can be fixed. There are workable solutions to understanding one another, communicating better, and helping to steer our children in the proper direction.

Chapter Five

When Anger Runs Deeper

WILL NEVER forget the way Diane and Craig looked the first time we met in my waiting room. Tired and frightened, their expressions and posture both spoke of defeat, and as they introduced their four-year-old son, I immediately discovered why. When I stooped down to shake young Robby's hand, instead of accepting the greeting, he punched me in the throat, stepped back and held up a threatening finger.

"You're not gonna fix me," he threatened. *"I'm* in charge."

Craig grabbed Robby's hand, and Diane cried. "We go through this all the time," she said. "We love our son, but he's destroying our family."

Indeed, there are children who get angry, and then there are children who live *very* angry lives. Robby was such a child. His wrath could cast a pall over any outing, monopolize the family's energies, and cause destructive conflicts between his parents.

Robby wasn't merely a grumpy child who sulked when he didn't get a toy. This was a child whose aggression was out of control. Children like Robby turn misunderstandings into meltdowns. While it may be hard to believe that children even this young can act this way or utter such nasty remarks, believe me, they can.

Real Cause for Concern

In previous chapters we've looked at children whose anger has become a destructive force in their own lives and in the lives of those around them. The focus of this chapter is on children whose anger is really off the normal scale, or is at least showing risk factors for escalating. Anger is destroying the quality of life of these children and their families, and in some extreme cases, taking our children from us at early ages.

Anger that persists despite your attempts to change it, is fearfully strong, and does not seem to be precipitated by reasonable causes may be due to an underlying emotional disorder of a more serious nature. Depression, bipolar disorder, and attention deficit disorder are among the more common diagnoses associated with anger. These illnesses make the treatment of anger more difficult, especially if the underlying problems are not identified. Anger and irritability, however, can be very real although often overlooked symptoms of these disorders. For example, as many as 30 to 40 percent of depressed adults have attacks of anger.[2] Anger and irritability are also common features of attention deficit disorder and bipolar disorder in children.

Some children with combined anger and emotional problems rarely have "good times," as they walk around under a perpetual storm cloud of menace and rage. Many others are withdrawn and can be secretive about their activities, which can be especially dangerous in households in which the adults, eager to avoid yet another hostile confrontation, leave their children to their own devices rather than meddle. We've all seen the tragic consequences of the extremes of this problem when sullen loners are allowed to create hate-mongering websites, spew bile into journals or writing assignments, or accumulate arsenals of weapons. All too often their parents had no idea what occupied their time, for they were grateful that their children weren't unleashing their venom on siblings or parents. Sometimes they didn't even know the extent of their child's venomous thoughts and feelings. But while such a hands-off policy, or in some cases downright ignorance of the true situation, may seem to keep the peace, in fact it can have catastrophic results.

Sixteen-year-old Lee is an example of the link between anger and emotional disorders. His classmates occasionally teased Lee about his Asian heritage. Not wanting to let his peers know they were getting to him, he acted like he was not bothered by the harassment, but at home, he would let out his frustration without telling anyone why. Instead, he complained his parents did not understand him and he retreated to his room where he played video games or just lay in bed. To avoid the other students, he dropped out of his afterschool activities. He started staying up through most of the night, which led to huge morning battles when his father tried to wake him for school. Being tired all day, Lee would fall asleep in class. Both his learning and his grades plummeted as he failed tests and stopped doing his homework. The fighting even spilled over to his brothers and sisters, as he became irritated over the smallest things.

Lee's parents refused to ignore the situation and took him to a psychiatrist who diagnosed him as depressed and prescribed an antidepressant medication and sleeping pills. In our counseling sessions, Lee explained to me that the quiet time at night was the only peace he felt all day. He was in a downward spiral of exhaustion, depression, and worry that he tried to treat by running away from the world. So he continued to resist going to school even if it meant more fights with the whole family.

One of the problems was that he never told anyone why he was avoiding school. As his depression grew, so did his inability to deal with even minor stresses. Later he told me "I was ashamed of who I was, ashamed I could not handle the teasing, ashamed I let things get this bad and was willing to fight against everyone so I would not have to admit I was a failure." It took a new school, new friends, counseling, medication, and getting his sleep schedule back on track before his anger began to settle down.

Although Lee's story had a happy ending, his violent outbursts were frightening. It is important to note, however, that the majority of children with emotional disorders do not resort to violence. But when they do, it is the stuff that we are all too familiar with in the headlines. Rates of violent crimes committed by teens have climbed considerably in the past fifteen years, boys tend to act with violence far more often than girls, and violence in childhood is one of the best predictors of violence in adulthood.[3]

But the vast majority of the tens of millions of schoolchildren do not lose control to that extent, and when they do, it tends to be provoked by a fight. Many of these youth offenders are acting out in violence that they learned from families or gang members, rather than acting out as a result of mental illness. If we concentrate only on the attention-grabbing headlines, we will miss a critically important point. Without taking away any of the seriousness with which we should approach youth violence, there is a larger number of our youth who suffer from a significant emotional disorder during their childhood years. These children are often forgotten in the shadows of the violent youth.

Anger and Depression

I remember the case of twelve-year-old Kevin. According to his mom, Colleen, he'd step off the school bus and literally drag himself up the front steps of his house like a prizefighter in his final, losing round. Inside, he'd snarl at his sister and resist his mother's efforts to engage him in conversation.

Rather than tolerate such poor behavior, Colleen would send Kevin to his room, but to no avail. His contrary mood got increasingly difficult each day, and he spent more and more time in his room, a marked change from his former routine of rushing out to play with friends. At mealtimes he picked at his food, and he didn't really participate as a family member. At first his mother thought it had something to do with the onset of adolescence, but he was also avoiding his friends. She thought his mood might also be a response to her divorce, but that had occurred five years ago. Colleen did remember, though, that over the years such a stress could resurface.

Fortunately, Colleen stayed connected with Kevin, and when he'd tell her to go away, it only strengthened her resolve to get at the root of the problem. The foul mood, the withdrawn attitude, the changes in eating and sleeping patterns, were all signs she paid attention to. In addition, she took the time to listen, and when she did, she found out that her son was struggling with friends at school, being ignored by a girl he liked, and wished his dad would call more often. Kevin felt overwhelmed, tired, and inferior to other kids in his class. Colleen was concerned that he was feeling more than just childhood sadness. She stayed alert to the signs of depression, even though such revelations were not easily accepted. Colleen may well have saved her son by focusing on the feelings behind his anger, rather than on the unpleasant impact his anger had on the family.

When dealing with angry or irritable children, it's important to consider the possibility of depression. Children do get depressed. In the past twenty-five years, researchers have noted that children can suffer symptoms of depression that are every bit as real as the manifestations in adults.

Almost 2½ percent of children and over 8 percent of teens in the United States suffer from depression.[4] In a given six-month period between the ages of nine and seventeen, about 5 percent of children suffer from major depression.[5] Although the recovery rate for a single episode of depression in children is very good,[6] depression during childhood can predict more serious illness in the adult years.[7]

Signs of Depression

In the case of Kevin, the irritability and sudden change in routine tipped off his mother to the very real possibility that something more than sadness existed. Each child might present different symptoms.

Anger is a signal that something is wrong. A well-known premise of psychology is that depression can be an expression of anger turned inward. While some kids are visibly irritable, even mean at times, others experience a change in sleep patterns and appetite, withdraw from friends and interests, and exhibit a sense of sadness overall. But, you might reasonably ask, aren't all children sad from time to time?

In fact, almost half of all children experience episodes of profound sadness, void of any joy, in any given year. Feeling a little blue is a common reaction to life's problems and doesn't necessarily mean the child is clinically depressed. The majority of children find ways to adapt to difficulties. Their sadness may be temporary until the cause of their sadness changes, or until they find a way to cope with their problems. For some children, however, their difficulties continue painfully despite their best efforts and coping skills.

Even after a child's problems disappear, her sadness may linger. When these symptoms last for a number of weeks, it's time to seek help. A popular misconception of depression is that such children are basically tired and sad. But the symptom picture is more involved.

The common symptoms of depression in children and adolescents include:

1. Persistent sad or irritable mood
2. Loss of interest in activities once enjoyed
3. Significant change in appetite
4. Oversleeping or difficulty falling asleep
5. Loss of energy
6. Feeling physically agitated or slowed down
7. Difficulty concentrating
8. Recurrent thoughts of death or suicide

Five or more of these symptoms must persist for two or more weeks for the diagnosis of depression to be indicated. According to the National Institute of Mental Health, there are several additional signs that may be associated with depression in children and adolescents:[8]

1. Frequent vague physical complaints
2. Frequent absences from school or poor school performance
3. Talks of running away from home
4. Outbursts of shouting, complaining, unexplained irritability
5. Being bored
6. Lack of interest in playing with friends
7. Alcohol or substance abuse
8. Social isolation
9. Increased irritability, anger, or hostility
10. Reckless behavior
11. Difficulty with relationships

Diagnosing depression in children is particularly difficult, because they are less skilled at communicating their feelings. Rather, they may tend to act out with irritability and anger, which, in turn, can be misread as a behavior problem. To better understand the possibility of depression, it is helpful to know more about how it affects children at different ages.

What's Normal Sadness? What's Not?

It can be difficult to distinguish between normal bouts of childhood sadness, irritability, and real depression. Depending upon the child's age, the signs will vary. Keep in mind, you should discuss any symptoms with your child's primary-care physician or pediatrician, who may refer you to a child psychologist or licensed social worker for another opinion.

YOUNG CHILDREN

Children of any age, including infants, school-age children, adolescents, and teenagers, can show signs of depression. It's difficult to think of an infant as being depressed because we imagine their lives as carefree. But youngsters do become depressed under some conditions. Prolonged separation from their parent, such as during a lengthy hospitalization, is one precursor. That's one reason hospitals place so much emphasis on parents' visits with their children.

When mothers and infants are separated for long periods, the child's reactions may come in three stages. A child may first seem to protest the separation with tantrums or other signs of frustration. He may then move into a stage of grieving marked by sadness. The third stage is one of detachment, where the infant doesn't seem to show emotions or appears quiet and unaffected by people. In extreme cases, an infant or toddler may develop a problem called "failure to thrive," in which he fails to gain, or even loses, weight. Failure to thrive can stem from complex problems between the infant and parent or may be caused by other health problems. It's not always related to separation, but it's important to realize that young children can and do suffer substantial reactions when away from a parent or guardian.

A depressed reaction can also occur in infants when a parent is emotionally very detached from their child. Jeff Cohen, Ph.D., a psychologist at the University of Pittsburgh, has studied the effects of mothers' postpartum depression on infants. This research is particularly important since as many as 10 to 20 percent of mothers suffer from this illness.

Cohen has found that depressed mothers will have fewer positive interactions with their infants, which may result in depressed behavior in the baby. The long-term effects, fortunately, are limited. As the mother improves, the baby gets better too.

AS KIDS GROW

Separation as the common cause of sadness or depression prevails in preschool and school-age children. Preschoolers are more likely to cling to a parent more after a death, a divorce, or at another significant time of family stress. School kids may withdraw from friendships or face a drop in their school performance. Depression not only affects emotions, but also impairs a child's learning and memory skills. Be sure to look for signs such as a withdrawal from extracurricular activities the child previously enjoyed, as well as increased irritability and anger. Above all, listen to what children tell you. When he's overly critical of himself and speaks with little self-confidence, it's a signal that he is feeling helpless.

TEENS, DEPRESSION, AND SUICIDE

Many teens are likely to experience feelings of depression during adolescence. Blame some of this on hormonal changes and moodiness, the shifting demands of their lives, or concerns over their own identity that result in turmoil. Suffice it to say, we need to have a solid network of supporters in the family, community, and schools to help teens cope during these troublesome years.

The conundrum in spotting a teen's depression is that most teens act a little moody, withdrawn, or unusual. It's part of being a teenager. But when we hear of suicide (or murder/suicide, as in some of the school violence), we react with shock.

Suicide among younger children is very rare, but among teenagers it's the third leading cause of death. In fact, many so-called accidents may have been suicide attempts. Depression doesn't always lead to teenagers taking their own lives, but any talk of suicide should be taken seriously, particularly if your child has recently lost someone close, especially another teen or young person who may have committed suicide. According to statistics kept by the National Institute of Mental Health, the strongest risk factors for suicide attempts in children are depression, alcohol or drug use, and aggressive or disruptive behaviors.

Watch with caution for signs of withdrawal, perpetual boredom, or emptiness. It is not uncommon for younger children or teens with no real concept of death's permanency to observe the fanfare surrounding a funeral with envy; in hopes of attracting the same kind of attention, they may think of ending their own life. Or they may harbor thoughts of joining a loved one in heaven.

Teen suicide is often committed to end intense pain and emotional suffering. Not all suicide cases show the classic signs of depression—just as all depressed kids don't contemplate ending their lives. But depression does put these children at greater risk. Other suicide risk factors include previous suicide attempts, substance abuse, eating disorders, psychosis, a history of suicide in the family or among friends, significant loss (death, divorce, abandonment), child abuse; poor academic, social, and family life; or sexual orientation problems.

Any child who utters phrases such as "I wish I were dead," gives away treasured belongings (as if preparing for death), or who engages in very dangerous behavior (playing with fire, drinking and driving, experimenting with drugs and unsafe sex) needs professional intervention *now*.

Depressed children and adolescents might also break the law in anger and defiance. Police officers attest to incidences of teens breaking windows, driving recklessly, or harassing ex-girlfriends or ex-boyfriends after a relationship breakup. Similar angry reactions follow other losses or stresses in a child's life. Again, they aren't always pure indicators of depression. But depression is often disguised by anger. Those who show a combination of anger and depression shouldn't be dismissed as simply having behavior problems that require more or stricter discipline. The behaviors themselves can be early warning signals, shedding light upon more serious problems.

Causes of Childhood Depression

Depression-related behaviors such as suicidal threats, declining grades, or sleepless nights can have complex causes. Three contributors to depression are emotional or physical trauma, biological causes, and learned helplessness.

Trauma

Trauma as a cause may be the death of a parent, a serious physical injury, or a poor grade at school. Not all children react to trauma in the same way, but a child's reaction should be taken seriously even if the event seems trivial. For example, an otherwise successful child can feel devastated by a poor grade on an important test.

Others may react intensely to the breakup of a relationship or to teasing by their peers. Their feelings are very real even if the event appears insignificant to adults. By the same token, some children barely react to events others find quite disturbing. When a child doesn't have a strong reaction to upsetting events such as death, abandonment, divorce, or a disabling injury, it doesn't necessarily mean she's handling the situation well. Showing neither sadness nor anger could be considered problematic. The trauma may manifest itself at another time, especially during adolescence, when the first stirrings of independence and the expectation of one day leaving the supports of home emerge.

Biological causes

Biological causes of depression stem from two sources—genetics and physical reactions to major stress. Depression does run in families. There could be a tendency toward, but not necessarily a cause of, depression that's inherited. When close relatives have a history of depression, the child's symptoms may relate to a genetic component that increases the risk for depression.

Persons who have faced traumatic events may undergo chemical changes in their nervous system that lead to depression. Chemicals called neurotransmitters (which send messages between nerve cells) may be altered by stress. These changes contribute to classic symptoms of depression such as sleep problems, appetite loss, and low spirits.

Learned helplessness

Third, learned helplessness leads to depression. When we face uncontrollable, emotionally painful events, we may later develop problems with motivation, thinking, and feeling. Children who face ongoing abuse, for instance, may feel powerless to stop the pain, and eventually they give up and endure it, seeing pain as an inevitable part of life. They don't have the experience of seeing their own behavior affecting their world in either a good or bad direction. They end up feeling hopeless and helpless. Children who have trouble adjusting to their physical disabilities may also experience this. They may even learn that by acting helpless, others will come and do things for them.

Treating a Child's Depression

Depression can often be worked through in counseling for the child and the family. For some children, however, treatment requires an additional component—medication. Mind you, medications aren't always required, and parents should be very cautious about rushing to the pharmacy. When it is prescribed, though, it's a good idea to continue counseling to help the child learn ways to deal with and overcome the depression.

Your child's physician, in conjunction with a psychiatrist or psychologist your child sees, will be pivotal in determining whether your child requires medication. Some parents ignore their child's symptoms, and refuse to broach the topic for fear they'll be stigmatized.

Several prominent people, such as former First Lady Rosalynn Carter, have fought valiantly for recognition that mental illness is no different than ordinary sickness. Organizations such as the National Association of Mental Illness (NAMI) have been working for years for the public to recognize mental illness as a very real and very biological problem.

Parents are sometimes apt to be wary of medicating their depressed children, viewing this still as a sign of weakness. Please understand that physical factors of depression can be as debilitating as any other physical malady such as diabetes or asthma. Taking medication doesn't mean that the child is bad, only that medication is required to help his brain function better, and in many cases it's used only for a short period of time.

Recognizing Attention Deficit Disorder

Even before he was born, Jeremy was giving his pregnant mother trouble. At a baby shower, his mother was resting a cup of tea on her abdomen. He gave a kick, which sent the saucer, cup, and tea flying. By age two he was getting into everything he could reach and scaling furniture to get at what he could not reach. By age four he was dismissed from his care center on the third day. When he entered first grade, his teachers noted how he would not keep his mind on his work or his hands to himself. By third grade he was battling with his parents over homework, as he would try to get up every few minutes to get a drink, play with the dog, or watch TV. Even when he did complete his homework, it would often be misplaced before it ever made it to the teacher's desk. His parents tried a whole host of punishments to keep him on track, but most resulted in tantrums and more fighting.

Jeremy had the characteristics of a child with attention deficit disorder, or attention deficit hyperactivity disorder, otherwise known as ADD and ADHD. (Following the terminology recommendation of the American Psychiatric Association, we'll use ADHD in this book, but do know that not all children have the hyperactivity component.)

This common but troubling disorder affects an estimated 5 to 6 percent of children, with boys far outnumbering girls in diagnosis. Very often it can be misdiagnosed, because there is no blood test or X ray that confirms the diagnosis. The true ADHD child may be mistakenly seen as a child who is immature, obstinate, or in need of discipline. Conversely, a normal child may be mislabeled as ADHD when the real problem is a learning disability, discipline, emotional stress, or overly high expectations (brought on by parents or perhaps even the child herself).

Anger and aggressive behaviors are frequently seen in children with ADHD. The combined symptoms are associated with greater psychological disturbance and possible substance abuse in later years.[9]

Because ADHD affects many children, it's important that every parent and educator understand the symptoms and the treatment of this disorder. Even if your own child isn't diagnosed with an attention deficit, chances are you'll know a child's friend, cousin, or classmate with the problem.

What Is ADHD?

Children with ADHD have difficulty concentrating, a short attention span, are easily distracted, and have impulsive tendencies. They may fidget during quiet activities and be overactive during active tasks. Many have diagnosable learning disabilities, and about 35 percent will require special education assistance. These children can be very difficult to manage at home or at school, and they are more likely than their peers to develop behavior problems and social difficulties.

The Causes and Impact of ADHD

No one knows the exact causes of attention deficit disorders. Many parents of ADHD children claim they had similar symptoms as a child, suggesting a genetic link. However, it's not always directly inherited.

Recent studies have suggested that their metabolism may be slower in certain parts of the brain that control attention and concentration. Much more work needs to be done before we clearly know the physical causes.

ADHD is not caused by immaturity of the child's nervous system, food additives, or bad parenting. Children who have suffered from brain injury, malnutrition, and traumatic psychological stress can show symptoms. Certain medications may produce side effects that mimic attention deficit symptoms, but these children aren't given the diagnosis of ADHD.

Signs first appear typically before a child turns six, and about half these children will subside in their symptoms by the time they are teenagers. For a child who is indeed diagnosed, problems with impulsiveness, inattention, and distractibility affect nearly every aspect of that child's behavior at school and at home.

Attention is essential to learning. Think of the steps in making a simple phone call. To make a call, we need to know with whom we want to talk, the spelling of their name, how to find their name and number in the phone book, remember the number, dial it, wait for the other person to answer, and then remember why we called them in the first place.

Most of us take these basic steps for granted, but if we get distracted along the way, we may end up dialing the wrong number or forgetting why we called. The child with attention deficit disorder deals with the interference of distractions in all he does. It's not that he is stupid or immature. He simply can't pay attention through all the steps necessary to learning and performing an action.

Such a child's mind may wander off frequently while the teacher is talking. She'll forget to write down the homework, and her distractibility pulls her mind away from studying or taking tests.

But their problems don't end in the classroom. These kids have trouble picking up the subtle social cues that tell them how to behave, even with their own friends. Thus, they'll come on too strong or seem to miss the point when talking or playing. One nine-year-old got into a fight with his friend the first day of school. The boy was running to greet his friend, misjudged how fast he was running, knocked his friend down, and a fight followed.

The actions of ADHD children in organized activities might also make them outcasts. During soccer games, Steven became the butt of his team's jokes because he was looking at dandelions instead of watching the game while the ball went flying by.

Diagnosing the Disorder

Typically, a team consisting of a physician (pediatrician, primary-care physician, or a psychiatrist), a psychologist, parents and teachers is assembled to diagnose a child with ADHD. The physician will carefully look for other possible medical causes. Again, there is no specific medical test to clearly diagnose the disorder.

The team will also look for psychological factors contributing to the child's demeanor or difficulties. The psychologist may administer tests to rule out any suspected learning disabilities. Parents and teachers fill out questionnaires or rating scales (for instance, the Conners scales), providing information regarding the child's history, symptoms, and performance in school and in social settings. Since children are often able to control their symptoms in new situations or when working one on one, their symptoms may not fully show up during the first office visit.

The symptoms of ADHD are divided into two categories: inattention and hyperactivity-impulsivity. The criteria to diagnose ADHD are listed below and are taken from the *Diagnostic and Statistical Manual,* which is the standard diagnostic guide for psychological disorders. Children must have six or more of the symptoms present in either category for a duration of at least six months. The behaviors must be to the level of often interfering with daily activities in two or more settings, must be inconsistent with the developmental level of the child, and must have their onset before age seven.

INATTENTION

- Fails to attend to details or makes careless mistakes
- Has difficulty sustaining attention in tasks or play
- Does not seem to listen when spoken to directly
- Has difficulty organizing tasks and activities
- Avoids tasks that require sustained mental effort
- Loses things necessary for tasks or activities
- Is easily distracted
- Is forgetful

HYPERACTIVITY-IMPULSIVITY

Hyperactivity

- Fidgets with hands or feet or squirms in seat
- Leaves seat during activities where sitting is expected
- Runs about or climbs excessively
- Has difficulty playing or engaging in quiet activities
- Acts as if driven by a motor
- Talks excessively

Impulsivity

- Blurts out answers to questions
- Has difficulty awaiting turn
- Interrupts or intrudes upon others

There is evidence that ADHD runs in families, which supports the presence of some genetic link. For example, there is a very high likelihood that if one identical twin has an ADHD diagnosis, so will the identical sibling. Similarly, the child often has another close family member with ADHD symptoms.[10]

Most children will begin to exhibit symptoms or signs during their preschool years. Unless the symptoms are rather severe, many parents will tolerate their child's behavior until it's pointed out by preschool, kindergarten, or elementary school educators. If you experience a concern, be sure to raise it with your child's doctor.

In diagnosing an attention deficit problem, it's important to evaluate what the child's problems are—as well as what they are *not*. Medical problems, learning disabilities, and emotional stress all mimic the symptoms of ADHD, just as inattentiveness can be caused by a straightforward visual problem. Likewise, a child who comes from a family with much abuse or who has an anxiety disorder will have a difficult time concentrating, but it's not a function of ADHD.

Children with ADHD symptoms related to learning or emotional problems should get treatment for their other difficulties and shouldn't receive the same medication or behavioral treatments that are used for a true ADHD child. For this reason alone, diagnosis is a complicated matter that should be carefully addressed by you and your physician.

In May 2000 the American Academy of Pediatrics issued its first guidelines for diagnosing ADHD, to ensure that merely rambunctious youngsters aren't overmedicated. This is important because there has been a dramatic increase in the use of stimulant medications, and the prevailing worry is that there's a rush to diagnose and medicate when other measures could provide a better first round of treatment. Under the new guidelines, a child must exhibit symptoms in at least two settings, such as in the home and at school, and these symptoms must interfere with a child's academic or social functioning for at least six months. That's why input from parents and teachers is crucial.

Treating Attention Deficit

While there is no cure for ADHD, there are treatments that reduce the symptoms, helping the family and the child cope. Two major treatments are behavior management and medication.

BEHAVIOR MANAGEMENT

I usually recommend the behavioral approach before a rush to medicate, unless one is dealing with severe symptoms. A psychologist or other mental health professional can provide behavioral help, with the goal of teaching children how to deal with their attention deficit problem.

Indeed, we can teach kids strategies to reduce impulsiveness and inattention. We can stress specific problem-solving techniques or methods of improving their organizational skills. For example, a child can learn to use the four steps of (1) setting a goal, (2) making a plan to reach the goal, (3) putting the plan into action, and (4) checking over their work to see if the goal was met and the plan correctly followed. Parents and teachers adapt techniques to deal with their ADHD children in ways that meet the child's needs. Programs often emphasize frequent feedback and clear rules to teach kids techniques for controlling their symptoms. All behavioral treatments, whether offered by mental health professionals in private practice or through clinic and hospital programs, should include training for parents in dealing with their child's problems.

One might reasonably ask how behavioral treatment for ADHD differs from traditional counseling and psychotherapy. Traditional psychotherapy alone aimed at treating emotional problems is generally not an effective treatment for the attention deficit disorder symptoms. Having said that, many of these kids develop other emotional and social problems that counseling might resolve. When there are multiple facets to a child's problems, a good therapist will use a treatment plan combining behavior strategies while concurrently addressing emotional concerns.

MEDICATION

About 90 percent of children with ADHD will receive medication at some time. Medications such as Ritalin, Dexedrine, Cylert, Adderall, Concerta, or Wellbutrin can only be prescribed by a medical doctor— your child's pediatrician, primary-care physician, or a psychiatrist. All but one of the medications I listed are stimulants (Wellbutrin is not), and you might ask why give a child who is hyperactive a stimulant. Research in people with ADHD has found their brain metabolism may be functioning slightly lower than for those without the disorder. The medication appears to stimulate important areas of the brain to function at better levels, especially those parts that control attention skills.

Bear in mind that medication does not make your child's ADHD symptoms disappear, and in many cases a missed dose means the effectiveness stops. Stimulant medications work fairly quickly, which is why many children receive an afternoon dose, administered by the school nurse. Antidepressants (which may have potential for treating some ADHD children) take longer to become effective; it may take thirty days before you start to notice any results.

Depending upon the medication prescribed and your child's symptoms, he may require doses only on school days, especially if he is taking one of the stimulant drugs. However, if your child's symptoms negatively affect social relationships and behavior, his doctor may recommend remaining on the medication every day.

Of course, medications can have side effects, including reduced appetite, headaches, abdominal pain, tics (motor and vocal), insomnia, and a change in heart rate or blood pressure. Some children suffer allergic reactions to their medication. If a prescription does not agree with your child, consult your physician and, of course, read the literature provided by the pharmacy so you know what to anticipate. Any potential side effects must be weighed against the positive outcomes of the medication, but the mere existence of side effects means that medication should never be dispensed cavalierly.

What Lies Ahead?

Children with an attention disorder can overwhelm their parents and teachers in the classroom. But there are ways of dealing with the disorders, and with practice and patience you too will improve in helping your child.

Most ADHD children should be in the regular classroom unless they have learning disabilities or behavior disturbances that require special assistance. Teaching methods might have to be adapted to the child. Thus, it's essential to keep the lines of communication open between parent, teacher, and other educators. Extra effort paid to the child and his studies early in the school year can prevent more extensive (and expensive) problems.

Kids with ADHD will grow up to lead very happy and productive lives. They are not destined for anything less. But they may have to work harder at certain tasks than their peers. Sometimes, a child's symptoms lessen with age and with the proper behavior management approach. Other times, a child with an attention disorder grows into an adult with the same problem. Children with a mixture of ADHD and anger may have a more difficult prognosis, rendering early diagnosis all the more important.

Certainly, if you have concerns about your child's inattention, distractibility, high activity level, and impulsiveness, seek treatment. Stay involved, for despite the frustrations of raising an ADHD child, parents make such a tremendous difference, contributing to greater happiness and success.

Tips for Parents with ADHD Kids

Parents who make even a simple request such as "Go get ready because we're leaving soon," may find a barefoot child playing outside ten minutes later. Here, the parents have to take some ownership of the problem.

Directions such as the one above are often too vague for the child with attention disorders. As parents become more skilled, they'll learn how to communicate with their child in ways that get the message across effectively. Here are some tips:

• **Be specific.** If you want your child to get his black shoes and blue socks on, tell him to do just that. "Go get ready" is simply too vague for the child whose mind tends to wander off.

- **Be direct.** Just as we react better to positive statements than criticisms, the child with ADHD will respond to your telling him what to do versus what not to do. A statement like, "And don't play with your video games when you get up to your room," will only distract your child into doing the very thing you don't want him to do.
- **Keep it brief.** In time you'll know how many tasks your child can focus on. But generally, the shorter the list the better. If you rattle off a sentence filled with four or five different to-do items, your child may very well be overwhelmed. Avoid lectures since these are distracting as well.
- **Pay attention to time.** Let your child know how much time she has left to do a job. Time reminders provide structure, which these children need a lot of. Time reminders, in essence, keep the child on task. Also, if you need to have something accomplished right away, tell your child "now." Avoid giving an hour to do a one-minute job just because you're used to him dawdling that long.
- **Use cues.** When talking to your child, make sure you have her complete attention. Ask her to look at you (not the TV). Try to prompt her attention with brief phrases like, "Listen." Have your child repeat back to you what you've requested. This further reinforces the directive.
- **Give reminders.** These can be checklists posted prominently in the house or in the child's school notebook. Also, use verbal reminders that aim toward getting your child back on task. Avoid distracting statements such as "What are you doing?" or "How many times do I have to tell you?" These will set the child's mind off in the direction of the question, not the focus of what you want him to be doing. Thus, say "Look at your paper" or "Make sure you put away all of your toys." Or ask a question such as "What is the next step in your homework?"
- **Praise often.** No one responds well to a constant litany of negative remarks, so keep your messages positive. If your child completed a task well, say so with a kind word. If she's made a mistake, tell her briefly, but directly. Insulting remarks will not only distract but make the child frustrated and angry.

- **Help but don't hinder.** Children with attention difficulties may have a hard time focusing on homework or sticking to their studies. They may yearn for breaks, but let these breaks be rewards for time focused on a task. Figure out how much focused time your child can handle, and use a break (to relax for ten minutes or to have a snack) positively. If your child keeps drifting off, hold off on the break. However, an important caveat here is to remember that ADHD kids have a hard time making the transition from unstructured free play with gross motor activity to the quieter, intense activities such as studying. (For more hints on homework hassles, turn to that section in Chapter 9, "Winning the Daily Battles".)

- **Be patient.** Raising a child with an attention deficit disorder requires a tremendous amount of patience and energy. You and your child may anger more easily. Support groups comprised of similar parents may encourage you through difficult times and expose you to new techniques that have proved successful for other families. In this age of the Internet, there are groups on-line, as well as the popular group CHADD (Children & Adults with Attention Deficit/ Hyperactivity Disorder). See Recommended Resources for contact information.

- **Communicate with teachers.** Become your child's active advocate. Ask to have him seated at the front of the classroom, where it's less distracting. Ask for weekly feedback, especially when monitoring medication. Encourage your child to write questions on paper, to curb the urge to blurt out questions or thoughts. This teaches patience.

- **Adapt your habits, thus helping theirs.** Kids with ADHD have a harder time making the transition from active to more passive activity. In other words, moving from gym to art class is tough. Couple that with the fact that Americans are being trained by television and video games to respond to rapid-fire scenes. Do your best to curb this onslaught of rapid-fire living. Encourage reading. Tune into documentaries. Turn off the Nintendo.

Other Disorders

While I've discussed depression and attention deficit disorders, there are a few other diagnosable concerns that arise when children externalize their problems.

Oppositional defiant disorder (ODD) is characterized by a pattern of negativism, hostile and defiant behavior that lasts at least six months. This occurs in a child who frequently loses his temper, argues with adults, defies the rules, deliberately annoys others and blames them as well. This child acts resentful, is overly sensitive, and is sometimes very spiteful. You may say that most angry children act this way. However, the child with ODD suffers these symptoms to the extent that they impair normal social, academic, or occupational functioning. Those with ODD typically externalize within the family, by challenging house rules or by being oppositional at home.

Conduct disorder is a more serious problem than oppositional disorder. Conduct disorder is marked by a lingering pattern (usually twelve months or more) of aggression to people or animals, destruction of property, lies and threats, and serious violation of established rules, which again impairs functioning in the social, academic, and job-related realms. When we say aggression, we mean a child who initiates fights, bullies, uses weapons, or forces sexual acts. We're talking about a child who has purposely set fires or broken into someone's property with the intent of causing destruction, or the child who shoplifts. And when I say violating established rules, I mean more than the typical teenager pushing the limits of the curfew. This is perhaps a young child (preteen or elementary age) who stays out all night, runs away, or skips school. Kids with conduct disorder expand their oppositional behavior beyond the family, challenging school rules or societal expectations.

Bipolar disorder, sometimes referred to as manic depression, is characterized by mood swings from high energy and elation to depression. At one time this disorder was thought to be very rare in children. However, recent findings suggest it may occur more often than we think, in part because the early symptoms are misdiagnosed. It is difficult to recognize in children because the symptoms resemble other mental disorders. Attention deficit disorder, oppositional defiant disorder, depression, and anxiety are a few of the labels placed on some children who later turn out to have bipolar disorder.[11]

Bipolar disorder occurs in about 1 percent of adults, and it's not clear yet how many children show early signs of the illness. Those who are later diagnosed as bipolar have been described by their parents as children who may have been very clingy, had uncontrollable tantrums and intense rages even as toddlers.

The manic periods may last from hours to days, with symptoms including extremely irritable mood, destructiveness, decreased sleep, talkativeness, feelings of racing thoughts, distractibility, and increased activity. Symptoms for the depressive episodes may include sadness and crying, difficulty falling asleep or too much sleep, irritability, a drop in grades, appetite changes, withdrawing from activities, and suicidal talk.

The onset of puberty can be a trigger for the illness, although symptoms may appear much earlier. Many children with this disorder are susceptible to drug and alcohol abuse. There is an inherited component to bipolar disorder. When one parent has the disorder, the risk for the child increases to 15 to 30 percent. When both parents have the disorder, the child's risk is 50 to 75 percent.

Although bipolar disorder is considered a serious illness and there is no known cure, the symptoms are very treatable with medication, support, and counseling. If you suspect your child could have bipolar disorder, consult your pediatrician.

Substance abuse. Youth who show symptoms of sleep pattern changes, irritability, deceit, and plummeting grades could be involved with drug and alcohol abuse. They may have been secretly experimenting with drugs months before you notice any symptoms. The key here is to be vigilant of any signs of drug use and get help right away.

When Anger Turns Deadly

Following school massacres, reporters have focused on truly out-of-control kids who may (or may not) have diagnoses of **antisocial personality disorder**. Not all people who kill fit the diagnostic criteria. However, when you suspect a child has a much deeper disregard for the rights of others, see a failure to conform to social norms with respect to lawful behavior, and witness acts that are clearly grounds for arrest or criminal prosecution, the entire family may require extensive help.

Those with a diagnosis of antisocial personality disorder are generally beyond the teen years but showed signs of conduct disorder before age fifteen. They have patterns of deceitfulness (repeated lying, conning others for their personal gain, or use of aliases), impulsivity and failure to plan ahead, irritability and aggression (as indicated by repeated fights or assaults), reckless disregard for others' safety or their own, consistent irresponsibility (repeated failure at work or in meeting financial obligations), and a genuine lack of remorse (rationalizing the hurt they've caused, their mistreatment, or acts such as stealing). These kids may be cruel to animals, display disregard for the law, and show a lack of empathy. While hostile aggressors might feel sorry after an impulsive act, antisocial aggressors don't feel at all. In fact, one could say they are emo-

---

Characteristics of Antisocial Personality Disorder

- patterns of deceitfulness
- impulsivity and failure to plan ahead
- irritability and aggression
- reckless disregard for others' safety or their own
- consistent irresponsibility
- genuine lack of remorse
- cruelty to animals
- emotionally numb or dead inside unless caught

---

tionally numb or dead inside unless they get caught. Strangely enough, these same youth often have a keen sense of injustice when they, themselves, are involved. They may not be sorry for the crime, but they feel resentful for doing the time. Kids displaying any of these traits may or may not be diagnosed with antisocial personality disorder. Regardless, they need intervention, and fast, before they become kids who could kill.

Hope Ahead

In the aftermath of several recent and much-publicized episodes of school violence, the Associated Press reported a surge in younger patients seeking help from mental health clinics and therapists across the country. While it is unfortunate that these tragedies were necessary to get people to pay attention to their children, it's indeed one element of good that has stemmed from utter despair.

Thus, if you take away anything from reading this chapter, let it be a twofold message. First, listen to your child—to his words, his actions, and his symptoms, which may signal something more serious. Second, know that there is reason for great hope. Whether it's an attention disorder, a learning disability, a behavioral concern, depression, or another psychiatric disorder, rest assured there are people who *can* help with appropriate treatments. As the adult most concerned for your child's well-being, you must deal with any signs you recognize. Facing dire consequences that might result from your denial would be far worse.

Chapter Six

Media and Society Messages

B Y THE time the average child turns eighteen years old, she will have spent 11,000 hours in school—and more than 15,000 hours watching television. This doesn't include time spent playing video games, when a child may perpetrate countless acts of mayhem, nor the hours spent surfing the Internet into areas of violence, pornography, and other unknown terrain. In fact, in 1998 electronic games were the second most popular form of home entertainment, following—you guessed it—television. Where do these statistics leave us as a society, and most important, what influence does media have on our children?

Media can expand our view of the world and help us look inward to enrich ourselves. Films and TV shows can demonstrate the power of love and hate, envy and acceptance, generosity and greed. Video games, websites, and Internet chat rooms and message boards can do the same. All can be avenues to learn about the complexities of life, morality, and good judgment.

However, as you've probably witnessed countless times, they can also portray life as filled with superficial problems with superficial solutions, whether they be violent or just plain silly. Some fear that freedoms will be taken away with restrictions or labeling of content. I see it as embracing the freedom we already have to make important choices and steer our children in healthy directions.

Teach your son or daughter to be cognizant of words and actions. In this era of worries about school violence, even a thoughtless uttering of "I'll kill you" sounds an alarm in the minds of fellow students and school faculty, who years ago would have shrugged off such a statement. Part of growing up is learning subtle cues of proper behavior.

It's not easy as a parent to decide what is okay for your child to be exposed to and what is not. But keep in mind the recurring refrain of this book when you struggle to evaluate videos, computer games, or the music your kids enjoy. It's sometimes okay to be angry, but it's never okay to be mean. It may be perfectly reasonable to show an angry character in a fictional plot, but we're sending a confusing message if we condone that anger when expressed as meanness, mayhem, or destruction.

In 1999 the American Academy of Pediatrics recommended that children under two years old not be allowed to watch television, that older kids not have television sets in their bedrooms, and that pediatricians ask parents to fill out a "media history," as well as a medical history, during office visits. Why? Because when children watch television, chances are good they are not getting enough of the other stimuli and activity necessary for proper development. Media violence also entered into the academy's stance.

According to the American Psychological Association, "There is absolutely no doubt that higher levels of viewing violence on television are correlated with increased acceptance of aggressive attitudes and increased aggressive behavior."

Identifying the causes of aggression and reducing it and other inappropriate behavior in our nation are of particular importance to health care professionals who must treat the wounds, both physical and psychological, that result. In the past thirty years, violence has replaced accidents as the number-one killer of kids. Teenagers are approximately two and a half times more likely to be victims of violent crimes than they were twenty years ago.

I'll discuss the age-old debate as to the effects of violence in a moment. But if the violent material our children are exposed to contributes, even in a small way, to the violence that manifests itself in real life, then knowing what our children are up to is worth our scrutiny.

The Impact of Real-Life Violence

While politicians and TV executives continue to argue the question of reducing TV violence, over two hundred studies tell us there is reason to be concerned. Even discounting those with flawed methodology, this research overwhelmingly backs up what we intuitively suspect: Children with impressionable minds are influenced by messages they see again and again.

To understand the influence of violence seen on television or in the movies, it helps to review first the impact of real-life violence on a child's behavior. Children who have been physically abused are more likely to exhibit aggressive and violent behavior than other children. Even witnessing abusive behavior has an impact on children; studies have shown that boys exposed to family violence have emotional and behavior problems akin to those of boys who have themselves been physically abused. Children who witness physical violence in their homes have an increased tendency toward assaultive behavior, suicide, homicide, and date rape. They are at two and a half times greater risk of developing psychological and behavioral problems than children who don't grow up in that environment.

The effects of witnessed violence extends outside the home. Dr. Bruce Perry has studied the effect on children of growing up in violent neighborhoods in Chicago. These kids exhibit signs of post-traumatic stress disorder, much as victims of domestic violence and combat veterans do. Repeated exposure to neighborhood or domestic violence can alter children psychologically, making them more impulsive and certainly more aggressive.

The Ongoing Debate

Since real-life exposure to violence affects children, it's not much of a logical leap to suspect that similar factors operate when violence comes in the form of glorified and fantasy depictions on TV, in the movies, on the Internet, and in video games. One of the earliest studies on this subject was conducted by Alfred Bandura at Stanford University in the early 1960s. He found that children who had viewed a film of an adult punching an inflatable doll were more likely to imitate the aggression when left with the same doll than were children who didn't see the film.

Anecdotal evidence from parents and teachers, as well as formal research, support the amazing influence TV has over children. Ask any parent or caregiver whether he notes differences in the behaviors of a child who watches a steady diet of "Mister Rogers' Neighborhood" and one weaned on "Power Rangers."

Links have also been found between television and suicide. One researcher monitored the content of soap operas and the national incidence of suicide rates for a six-year span. Within three days of a major soap character committing suicide, there were significant increases in suicide rates among women in the country.

And it's not only the incidence of aggressive or self-destructive behavior that seems to be aggravated by messages in the media, it's that kids learn to expect instant gratification because they're told the "good life" requires clothing, toys, or electronic equipment, and they're more conscious than kids a generation ago of labels. They believe all their happiness, overall satisfaction, and sex appeal later on depends upon Brand X instead of Brand Y. Fitting in becomes a matter of what we own, rather than who we are, and it's no surprise that children, especially young teens who are still exploring their own identities, are highly susceptible to such media manipulation.

As parents, we must help children make sense of the media messages they see. When parents monitor what children watch, and talk about aggression, violence, or suicide when it occurs, kids can keep such behavior in proper perspective. They need to be told that problems *can* be solved without hurting someone or hurting oneself.

What I'm saying here is three-pronged. First, there is an increased tendency to act aggressively and a decreased tendency to use calmer and more thoughtful approaches to problem-solving after exposure to violence. Second, witnessing countless acts of violence either from real-life experience or passively through the media leads a child to believe that violence is more prevalent—and acceptable—than it really is. Third, television viewers are so bombarded by watching violence that their responses to such acts have become dulled, causing those who produce such content to up the ante with greater violence and higher body counts.

Mix in More Technology

Much has been said and written about video and computer games as especially insidious influences. The counterargument that such games enhance a child's ability to solve problems, test hypotheses, decode information, and most likely sharpen their hand-eye coordination pales against the growing body of evidence supporting the theory that violent video games alter a child's natural inhibitions against killing.

Take a look at the advertisement for a video game called *Subspace*. "Meet people from all over the world, then kill them," it reads. Ad copy from the game *Point Blank* offers "more fun than shooting your neighbor's cat." How can this be good for children whose attitudes, sensitivities, and values are still in the formative stages?

The child who watches violence on TV is a passive viewer. Video games, on the other hand, require action on the child's part. Often he has to choose, at least symbolically, to kill or attack an opponent hundreds of times in a game. The more mayhem he creates, the higher his score. Physiological reactions such as increased adrenaline levels also add to the thrill.

Still, does exposure to screen violence lead to violent behavior? We do know that violent video games were a common thread in at least two of the five school shootings that occurred between 1996 and 1999. Theories abound on each side of the video game debate.

David Walsh, a child psychologist and founder of the National Institute on Media and the Family, believes there is cause for concern regarding video games. Interviewed for a *Time* cover story following the Columbine, Colorado, school massacre incident, he reported that the technology behind most of these games is based upon the psychological principle called "operant conditioning." Essentially, players are stimulated, they respond, and they are rewarded.

"Research has shown that operant conditioning is a powerful shaper and influencer of behavior," Walsh told *Time.* "The obsession is not about violence; it's about how engrossing the game becomes."

Engrossing these games are, to such an extent that children become addicted to electronic gadgets. Some can no longer amuse themselves and pass time the way children have for ages—by reading, playing board games, building things, and enjoying sports (which is sorely needed, since children are leading a more sedentary lifestyle).

Another educator takes a similar stand. David Grossman taught psychology at West Point and now serves as an adjunct faculty member at Arkansas State University in Jonesboro. He believes that violent games such as *Doom* help break down our inhibitions. Indeed, as games have evolved since their first introduction, the targets have gone from aliens and monsters to human targets, which become more lifelike with improved technology.

A study done at the University of Missouri found a relationship between long-term violent video game playing and aggression/irritability in children.[12]

Not surprisingly, the video game industry disputes the correlation between real violence played out in schoolyards, homes, and streets, and the products they manufacture. Company spokespeople point to their own studies linking youth violence with factors such as poverty, lack of parental involvement, mental illness, access to guns, and substance abuse. Experts who believe the impact of these ultraviolent games on the mentally healthy is virtually negligible. Still others, including those who actually play violent games, see it as merely a release, not a rehearsal for future tragedy. But for a child in a precarious emotional state due to the myriad factors discussed in other chapters, these games may be sending a message that violence and anger are not just acceptable, but a goal.

Recent scientific reports underscore the impact of learning on the brain during the early teen years. Although most brain development occurs before age six, evidence suggests that learning patterns during the pre- and early adolescent years influence the development of permanent paths in the brain as well as loss of pathways that are not used. In other words, this is a critical and influential time in brain development. And it begs the as-yet-unanswered question: Does the repeated rehearsal of even symbolically violent behavior (video games and TV) have long-term biological impact upon the child?

The Advent of the Internet

Television and video games are not the only sources of negative imagery that our kids are exposed to. In 1998, seventeen million kids between the ages of two and eighteen were on-line, and that number is expected to more than double in just five years. Like most innovations, the Internet has a lot of good going for it. But those I've treated have made me realize that it's also laden with drawbacks.

I still remember the fifteen-year-old boy from a rather affluent suburban school who came to a therapy session one day with a computer disk in hand. "Take a look at this stuff I downloaded off the Net," he said. The disk contained pages of instructions for making bombs. Our discussion revealed that he spent endless hours exploring sites with very questionable content on the computer in his room. His mother had no idea what he was up to, since he could quickly change the screen whenever she came into his room. Of particular concern to me was the casual fascination with which he described his treks into sites filled with sex and violence. Eventually, this boy's parents moved the computer from his room to the kitchen, installed an Internet filter, and restricted his on-line time. Although he fought these changes, his parents noticed how much calmer he became after only one week away from these sites. Parents must *not* rely on their child's judgment to decide if a site is appropriate or not. In this boy's case, he was becoming increasingly tense and rebellious. His computer use was reaching addictive levels, causing him to stay up late, miss sleep, skip homework, and lie about what he was doing—all signs that should trigger a parent's concern and lead to intervention.

Another unsettling element of the Internet culture is the uncertainty of who else is on-line. At least when your teenager is chatting endlessly on the telephone, you have faith they're talking with a friend. On the Internet it's conceivable that fourteen-year-old Sally, told that her chatmate is fifteen-year-old Hannah, is really sharing her life with forty-nine-year-old Harry. I don't think any of us wants a scenario such as this to influence children.

How Have Things Gotten So Out of Control?

Parents, educators, health professionals, and certainly legislators like myself struggle with how to reconcile our desires to curb violence and foster healthier attitudes with an individual's rights to privacy and free speech. Legislation such as the Telecommunications Act of 1996, requiring that new televisions come equipped with a V-chip that allows parents to program out objectionable material, is a step in the right direction. Movie, game, and music producers can step up voluntary efforts to raise standards. But parents—not the federal government—are the best gatekeepers for their kids.

It's not enough merely to check children's CDs for parental warnings or forbid them to see R-rated movies that you feel contain unsuitable material. Even seemingly benign or neutral media content may be fraught with unwanted material messages.

Sit down and watch television with your kids, and as you do, ask yourself if the main characters are modeling the kind of behavior or respectful attitudes you expect in your home. Does your child have the maturity to understand that the mouthy, precocious kids in her favorite sitcom are fictional characters, and can she enjoy it for the entertainment value without taking on the characteristics you abhor? Witness how situations in the programs you share are resolved. Do the characters use common sense and compassion, or anger, manipulation, deception, and hostility? Do they show respect for each other, or engage in a constant barrage of sarcasm, insults, and questionable morals? If the characters lived next door, would you trust them to baby-sit your children? Would these characters be welcome on a family vacation? If the answer is no, then it's time to change the channel. Otherwise, think of the impact these characters could have on the development of your child's behavior and values.

We must also monitor what we take for granted, including the evening news. Live remotes and television news teasers literally bring violence into our living rooms. Although older children can often differentiate between what happens elsewhere and in their own neighborhood, TV news can be very frightening for children younger than nine years of age who can't readily distinguish between reality and fantasy. When viewing unsettling news of kidnappings, accidents, or killings, kids need our presence to allay their worst fears.

Parents—the ultimate filters—must actively monitor their children's recreation, the influences they are exposed to, and discuss openly the less laudable aspects of the entertainment industry today. Many young kids follow the fads of preteens or older teens, not understanding that the music the "in crowd" talks about ad infinitum is actually contrary to their own and their family's values. It's the parents' job to help them recognize that the imagery depicted in music, art, books, television, and movies has literal as well as figurative meaning, and that there are many ways to evaluate these media. Help them evaluate how these meanings jibe with their own personal codes of conduct, and find alternatives if necessary.

Is Vigilance Synonymous with Snooping?

Some parents genuinely have a hard time monitoring their children's television or computer usage, as they liken it to eavesdropping or an invasion of privacy. This has a certain validity, as even children are entitled to express private thoughts to a friend or even to themselves, as in a diary. But while you are likely to know your child's telephone buddy, you don't know for certain who is at the other end of a computer connection. And unlike a book or a magazine, the Internet has no built-in editor, no publisher, no censor of the material your child could access.

Parents recognizing this distinction have several options. First, they can discuss the need for discretion with their children as a safety measure. Kids—and adults, for that matter—should refrain from divulging any personal details over the Internet. This includes street addresses, school or church locations, where they hang out, or their full names. Kids should *never* post their pictures on public sites, especially when combined with identifying names, nor should their relatives. Avoid filling out "questionnaires" with personal details, even if it appears to be going to a friend. Not all Internet information is secure, and often it can be viewed by strangers. Let your youngster know that giving away too much information is the equivalent of taking candy from a stranger or getting into an unfamiliar car.

If you know your child's computer screen name or nickname, you can check what's being said by or about them using Internet search engines that allow you to type in a screen name and find links and postings on

Internet message boards. Parents can also opt for filters barring access to dangerous or blatantly offensive material, and monitor where the computer's browser has been browsing. Most families report that their service providers do filter out questionable material in "kids only" accounts. This may mean that when your high school sophomore is writing a paper on breast cancer, drug abuse, or sexually transmitted diseases, the information she needs will likely be blocked because of the words "breast," "drugs," or "sex." In those cases, you'll have to work with your child, assisting in the research, but it's worth the ounce of caution. Otherwise, your child may be the unwilling recipient not only of pornographic e-mail enticing them to unsavory websites, but get-rich-quick schemes and credit card offers that are equally inappropriate. You may also want to look into kids-only search engines, like Yahooligans.

Controlling what your child sees is far from easy. Joshua, a thirteen-year-old, was constantly battling his mother about his computer time. One of his clandestine activities was surfing the Internet for pornography. When his mother caught him, she declared the computer off limits for a week. His angry reaction, which included a threat to break the computer, lasted for several days. When he realized he was getting nowhere with his mother, he started to pick on his brother and sister. "He was like an addict going through withdrawal," his worried mother observed.

Once he got his computer back, she installed a program to filter out objectionable content, but Joshua found out the password and disabled the program. His mother tried another program that set time limits on the computer, but again, he disabled the program and would secretly log on at night. Finally, she made a rule that he could only use the computer when she was in the room. As before, he tried to intimidate her into relenting. This time, however, she added a new rule: As soon as he started to mouth off, the computer was turned off. She stuck with the rule and soon he started to calm down. What made this work was her recognition that he was so drawn to these temptations that she had to monitor him closely. It never would have worked if she had given him more chances to be on his own.

Suggestions for Monitoring the Media

· Rather than allot a certain amount of time to television, select viewing by the program. It's wise to turn off the television completely on school nights. In fact, since schools have cut back on physical education, and obesity rates among kids are on the rise, encourage them to get outside and get fit when homework is done rather than loll in front of the television or computer.

· Weekly limits work well for television and video game usage. At the beginning of the week encourage your child to read the TV listings to select programs that are truly important to them. You can steer your kids toward documentaries or news programs that might help in their studies.

· Always choose a program before channel surfing. Not knowing what you want to watch, and merely settling for whatever is offered, results in more TV time.

· Don't assume a show is appropriate for kids simply because it airs in the daytime.

· Create "no TV times" during meals, homework sessions, or when the weather is perfect for outdoor play.

· If TV is a motivator, let your children earn TV time by reading or engaging in less sedentary pursuits. This works well for children who put off reading. Tell them they can watch an hour's worth of television for an hour's worth of reading. You might just see more books devoured!

· Keep the television and computer in a public area of the house, not in a child's own bedroom or play space.

· Use your VCR to record shows you as an adult want to see but that your children have no business viewing, and watch them when your children are asleep or out of the house.

· Build a library of quality videos, material taped from television to view later, or computer games children will actually learn from. Young children especially love watching familiar material over and over again.

• Use the Internet to your advantage. Many music groups maintain websites today, so it's relatively easy to download or view lyrics to popular songs before your children beg for them at the mall. Discuss why you approve or disapprove of their favorites. Lack of parental advisories is no guarantee of the music's suitability for kids.

• Monitor Web downloads. Left to his own devices, your child might download songs or videos that you wouldn't allow him to buy in the store.

• Explain the hidden aspects of media messages. Even TV commercials can provide lessons on life. Ask your children to analyze whether the Olympic skater really eats the cereal he's hawking for breakfast or whether the toy really works like that when you bring it home. Explain camera angles, stunts, and how animation and technology achieve fantasy versus reality.

• Teach your children to question what's presented in commercials. Ask them to compare advertised and less expensive brands. Refuse to purchase products advertised on shows that glorify violence, and tell your children—and the manufacturers—that you are doing so. Write to game and television producers with your comments and feedback.

• Be an active viewer. Allow children to talk back to the TV rather than accept everything they see and hear as fact. Teach kids to find ugly, toxic content as repugnant as you do. Talk about better ways of conflict resolution than the violence depicted in the media.

• Counter violence with alternatives. If you do see violence reported on the nightly news, discuss how the situation could have been resolved peacefully. If it's portrayed in film or in games, talk about whether it was necessary to the plot or merely added as gratuitous carnage.

For most children, casual exposure to violent imagery in the media will not interfere with their ability to develop respectful, humane outlooks on life. And different children can be affected in different ways by the same program. But it's a parent's job to be vigilant and know your child. Watch your child for signs that violence may be leaving an unwanted mark on her personal moral code. After playing Nintendo, does your child carry the aggressive behavior over to her daily interactions? Is she mean, rough, or disrespectful of others (adults or peers)? Does she exhibit aggressive, angry, or irritable signs that could be symptoms of anxiety or depression?

It can't be repeated too often that parents need to keep a connection with their children in order to understand them and have ongoing influence in their development. With television, video games, or computer usage, that means checking your entertainment preferences at the door occasionally and playing these games or browsing websites with your child that interest them, not you. This is the only way you can truly tell what tastes are emerging within your child, and if they don't meet with your approval, then you can engage in honest discussion and steer them to more appropriate matter.

Again, if your child seems obsessed with violent media, and if you concurrently see signs of failure at school, in relationships, or self-esteem, don't delay in getting help.

part 2

Strategies for Coping with and Preventing Anger

Chapter Seven

Arguments and Solving Conflict

I F I HAD to name a single complaint that drives more parents to seek my services for their children than any other, it would have to be a variation on this theme: "My child and I never stop fighting. Every suggestion, every request, no matter how calmly or benignly made, winds up leading to a rip-roaring, knockdown, drag-out argument. Sometimes we fight about fighting; sometimes we fight about nothing! But every time she opens her mouth, we end up arguing."

If you live with an angry child, no doubt you find yourself locked in verbal battles far more often than you would like. Perhaps you even avoid engaging your angry child in conversation for fear that the discussion will quickly derail, leading you both to part in a huff, slamming doors and muttering, "It's impossible to talk to you" or "There's no reasoning with you." Siblings too will go out of their way to avoid getting caught in the sticky web of the angry child's combative conversational style, figuring there is no winning anyway.

It's frustrating when arguing becomes the predominant mode of communication in your household, if for no other reason than it's not a particularly effective way to communicate. You rarely exchange information in a logical way, and in fact you might drag in superfluous facts that you already know, rendering the situation more confusing than before you began arguing. Certainly, arguing takes far more energy than calmer modes of discussion, and arguments up the tension ante, as all parties wait apprehensively for the boom to lower once again.

Angry kids tend to excel at creating arguments, sometimes out of thin air. Unfortunately, because they are *not* very good at problem-solving, the arguments they provoke are rarely productive. Starting a fight puts a child in charge, giving her a sense of power, especially if she sees you losing control of your emotions. When she senses she's starting to lose the fight, she feels the corresponding loss of that power. In order to regain it, she may resort to all sorts of dirty tricks in order to distract you from the matter at hand—resolving the point at issue and defusing the emotions on both sides.

This is not to say that arguments can never be productive. At their best, arguments can provide a forum for two individuals to air conflicting viewpoints—even over a matter as seemingly cut-and-dried as one's desire to eat a second piece of cake or another's need to use the telephone—and work toward a resolution that encompasses both their needs. But too often arguments fall into familiar patterns that have become ingrained over months and years of repetition. When this happens, the original complaint is soon forgotten as both sides fall into roles as tightly scripted as any Shakespearean drama.

Why Kids Argue

Kids have arguments for lots of reasons, and so do adults. So while it may be annoying to argue over seemingly petty things like chores or television, as the parent you need to remember it's less important *what* you and your child argue about than *why*. When one child might grumble but resignedly head off to bed at the appointed time, why will another insist that no child his age should be expected to adhere to such an unfair regulation? In fact, an angry child could work everyone into such a strung-out state that all family members fall into bed tired and teed off. *What* is behind such aggressive and contrary behavior? Getting to the heart of the *why* will help you deal most effectively with arguments when they arise.

We sometimes find ourselves arguing about the same things with our children, in the exact same way each time, and yet we wonder why the outcome never differs. I feel compelled to mention that one definition of insanity is doing the same thing over and over, and expecting different results.

Angry children have a very limited repertoire when handling difficult situations, so arguments tend to follow the same predictable patterns even though they inevitably lead to the same miserable outcomes. We need to teach angry children more effective ways to deal with problems than resorting to threats and meanness. This, in turn, gives them a route to achieve a more healthy self-esteem and helps them avoid future conflicts.

Arguments can be destructive or constructive depending upon your goal and your technique. They will also teach you to recognize the dirty tricks angry children often resort to in the course of an argument that actually *increases* their anger—and yours. By learning how to deal with these two factors effectively, parents can develop a road map instead of a battle plan. They can identify problems and detours to avoid the old traps that repeatedly yield harmful results.

What's the Point?

Angry children, it would seem, love to argue. Even though they can be nice when they want, if you deal with an angry child on a regular basis, you'll most certainly get into an argument before long. The argument doesn't have to make sense, or be about anything in particular, but you'll still find yourself caught in battle.

Stop and think about arguments you have had. With the perspective of time and distance, most arguments seem pretty stupid. Even when the issue itself is important, the way you handle it may be dumb. So, it's not just what you argue about, but the way you do so, that's important. When the topic or the techniques get out of control, ultimately everyone feels and acts worse.

When you find yourself getting into an argument, think about this question for a moment: What is your goal? The majority of people I've encountered say "to win." But when victory rather than problem-solving is the goal, certain patterns (not all of them helpful) tend to emerge.

Think about the last few arguments you and your child waged. What was your goal? Keep that goal in mind and compare it to the list below. After asking this countless times in counseling sessions and workshops, I've found most responses fall into one of six categories. Let's review to see what impact each goal has upon the argument's direction.

Typical Goals of Arguments

#1 To Win
#2 To Keep the Peace
#3 To Destroy
#4 To Vent
#5 For the Sport of It
#6 To Share Information
#7 To Solve the Problem

GOAL #1: TO WIN

When it comes to verbal sparring, the adage, "It doesn't matter if you win or lose, it's how you play the game," should be rewritten as, "It only matters if *I* win or lose." The matter at issue takes a backseat to the personal goal of coming out on top. Of course, the underlying tenet of this type of argument is, "I'm right and you're wrong," and the combatant with this goal will resort to a host of techniques to prove it. You or your child may try to intimidate, distort, or manipulate. You may use every trick imaginable to confirm that you do indeed know it all. Winning becomes convincing the other side, "I'm right, you're wrong, end of argument."

When winning is the goal, a person may keep on fighting even after he's figured out he's wrong. A child may even acknowledge later that he knew he was wrong but his goal was to see you surrender. Parents may find themselves arguing with a child who only wants to hear "Okay . . . you win" over everything else.

The problem with this goal is that it prevents the one intent on victory from listening to and learning from his opponent. Anyone who has argued with a child who wants to win for the sake of winning realizes the issue at hand is soon forgotten in the heat of battle. The result? Someone has to lose, someone feels frustrated or defeated.

When angry children focus on winning, they are focused on getting their way. So if the child wants to go out with his friends on Friday night, but his parents have stipulated that his room must be clean and homework finished, his goal will still be going out on Friday. Getting the work done probably isn't the goal, and the child will fight his parents' attempts at compromise.

Parents may hear excuses like, "But I already told my friends I'm going with them. I can't go back on my word . . . I'll clean my room later." Or, "Why should I clean it? Your stuff is a mess too." Even if these things are true, and they may well be, they don't address the issue at hand, which is the fact that the child has failed to meet the conditions previously agreed upon.

In such a situation, the angry child will try a battery of techniques until he finds an opening to put his mom or dad on the defensive. He may make threats, hurl accusations, or play the martyr to get them off their demand. Once he's done that, he wins.

In this case, winning might enable him to go out, but it won't help him do better with his schoolwork. Furthermore, the winning goal was counterproductive in that it reinforced his belief that when he fights, he gets his way. It rewards the anger.

GOAL #2: TO KEEP THE PEACE

One frustrated mother remembers an argument that arose when she asked her son to turn off the video game and start his homework. In fact, she had warned him a half hour earlier that he'd have to put the game away soon, but he'd conveniently forgotten. When she insisted he put the game aside, he yelled at her, "Now you made me mess up. I'll have to start over! And it's your fault if I don't have time to do my homework." Rather than start a huge confrontation, which could easily rage on for another half hour and result in no homework resolutions, she took the path of least resistance and let her son finish his game—just to keep the peace.

There are many families with an angry child in which parents avoid fights for just that reason. In some instances, parents may actually fear their child. After all, if you know you're going to face a major blowup, avoidance is a survival strategy. It may also be the way the parents handle conflict in other aspects of their lives—avoiding a fight at all costs.

Parents who themselves grew up in homes that were pretty volatile keep the peace as a learned means of self-protection. Perhaps they had an angry or domineering parent and learned early to get out of the way. One man told me he feared his own father so much that he and his siblings put up with anything just to avoid unleashing his father's wrath. Now he carries that same survival skill into the workplace, where he's learned to be peacemaker whenever tension builds among coworkers. At home, if a battle starts, he just lets the kids have their way rather than allowing things to erupt. Offer him peace and he'll do anything for you. Consequently, his children run roughshod over him, and his home is anything *but* the peaceful haven he sought.

Some parents take the easy road simply to avoid a sense of inadequacy. One parent told me she grew up an only child in a pretty happy home, so all the fighting with her three kids was new and stressful territory. When they fought, she thought she must be doing something wrong, and gave in to their demands in order to maintain tranquillity. This made her feel better as a parent. Not exactly logical, but she reasoned in her own mind that as long as there was no fighting, she must be doing something right. Wrong.

Still other parents retreat into a peacekeeping posture because their lives are already so filled with stress that they've reached the breaking point. The parent up to her neck with work tension may have little stamina to handle her children's squabbles. Thus, she'll shout at her spouse to give the kids what they want just to stop the arguing.

Whether the motivation is to avoid battles, fearful recollections from childhood conflicts, feelings of personal inadequacy, or being maxed out on stress, the results are the same: Children learn that as long as anger works, there's no reason to stop and every reason to keep it up.

Of course, it's important to note that we've all used this technique at times, perhaps with little tantrums. Keeping the peace may also be the right goal if you are in an abusive situation where fighting back would not be safe. However, if you need to use this goal for survival, make it a short-term goal, not an ingrained behavior.

GOAL #3: TO DESTROY

The worst arguments occur when your opponent's goal is nothing short of total destruction. There are no issues in this foe's mind other than your misery, no goal except your pain. This is when threats and anger hit the explosive stage; whether it's with a fist, a weapon, or words, the angry child only wants to hurt. Reason has no place in this kind of argument; the best thing you can do is protect yourself, and if possible protect your child from harm.

When faced with a barrage of words, focus your efforts on calming the child. Sometimes that means walking away. Sometimes that means speaking calmly and asking him to relax and regain control. In rare cases a child may even become violent.

If the attack gets physical, you may have to defend yourself by restraining your child. This is especially important if he's in a fit of rage and attacking you or another child.

All children have moments when they get so mad they may lose their temper. But when it's a habitual pattern, or if there is even one outburst so big that you feared for yourself and/or your children's safety, get help.

Children who use threats and physical attacks may intimidate their family if they seek help. I've often seen parents who, when confronted with their child's violent behavior outside the home, admit they could see it coming but felt paralyzed in the face of their child's anger.

But difficult as it is, we can't run from the truth. If your child's anger has reached the point where you genuinely fear he or she may harm you or someone else, you *must* reach out for help. Yes, your child may rage or even issue threats to retain a sense of control over you, but the alternative may result in worse consequences for others.

Over the years in my practice, I've had families that didn't bring their children back for treatment because the child threatened them with harm if they did. These are the children I worry about most, and I always urged such parents to keep the appointment; even without the child, if necessary. Such bullies want to protect their power and will sometimes turn up their threats when their power is weakened. Be assured, however, that such a child truly needs professional treatment, and will not relinquish his hold over his family without it.

In the most serious cases, professional intervention of another sort may be required. If your child's aggression is bringing harm to the family, you may need to contact the police for help. It's important to note that by doing so, you're not inviting the police to haul your child away to jail, but you can make them aware of a potentially volatile situation so they can protect you—and your child. It should go without saying that this option should be used only when there is actual danger of harm, *not* when you're having an argument. Well-trained police will follow up to see if your family is getting help.

Some children have been shocked that their parents would call the police, and have been frightened by the realization that their own behavior was so out of control. For some children this can be a wake-up call—that their parents are finally taking a stand. But a simple encounter with the police won't make your child change. Even if your child seems under control, the situation is not resolved. Follow through with getting help.

GOAL #4: TO VENT

We all have days where we're grumpy and short-tempered. We mutter under our breath about petty grievances, or we slam a door. Children have their share of bad moments too. Maybe they're tired or hungry or just stubbed a toe. Maybe they received a poor grade or had an unhappy experience with a friend. Whatever the reason, they're in a bad mood and just want to vent.

When a child walks around under a black cloud, virtually any-thing—or even nothing—can provoke an argument. If only we had some kind of warning system that would let parents know when that was the case, we could step away and come back later, when the child was calmer. Instead we may get caught in their venting and think it was something we did or said that caused the anger.

When you hear a child say "Leave me alone," sometimes the best thing you can do is just that. Give her a little space. If you can give time, give it. You don't have to talk things out at that moment, and if she's so upset she's venting, then a little time to relax could help a great deal toward meaningful conversation.

Later when you can talk with your child, get her to focus on the trigger feeling we learned about in prior chapters. There might be jealousy, pain, or sadness behind her anger, and you can help your child recognize these emotions without lashing out at those around her who have nothing to do with what's causing her upset. Granted, it may be hard, especially if your child rarely talks about feelings. But at least try to see what's going on in your child's mind.

Timing is also very important. Asking an angry child how he's feeling may only get you: "Quit being so nosy and leave me alone." Ask again later, when the child is calm, if he wants to talk about what's troubling him; you may get a more revealing answer.

If it's not possible to step back and allow a venting child to regain calm on his own, you may need to offer a gentle reminder. You could say: "I know you're upset that you didn't get invited to the party. I can understand you're feeling sad. But you can't take it out on your brother." This shows sensitivity, directs attention to the underlying emotion, and still sets limits. Again, you're telling your child that it's okay to be angry, but it's never okay to be mean.

We all give someone a little understanding when they've suffered a big disappointment—that's a good way to show sensitivity. In such instances a little venting can be excused. But don't forget to review the underlying reasons for the show of anger when your child reaches the aftermath stage. Yes, he may have had good reason to be upset when he found out he didn't make the team, but this doesn't excuse his picking a fight. Some parental discretion may be warranted in meting out discipline after an episode of venting, but a parent should never ignore a child's meanness. Reinforce the idea that there are boundaries of how we can act even when we're justifiably upset.

GOAL #5: FOR THE SPORT OF IT

I've often had parents complain that their angry children seemed to pick fights for absolutely no reason at all. They were convinced that they had missed a sign or some earlier hurt that caused their children to bedevil their siblings or be confrontational with their parents. In truth, there may not have been a sign to miss. Sometimes an angry child will go out of her way to start a fight for something to do. Just for the fun of it, kids will call each other names, tell the parents fibs to get the other in trouble, and break one another's toys—often for no other reason than they're bored and find torment enjoyable. This is the stuff of sibling rivalry that drives parents to distraction.

A parent might wish that kids would just learn not to do these things since they invariably result in tears, punishment, or negative feelings. But they won't learn on their own. They'll continue unless parents put their feet down. Without parental intervention, the situation can quickly get out of control, leading to physical and emotional bruises that build up for the next retaliation. Discipline when the unwarranted teasing and tormenting start. It also helps to involve siblings in activities to burn off some energy. My mom and dad had a favorite response when I rough-housed with my brothers and sisters. They said: "Since you have so much energy, how about cleaning the kitchen?"

GOAL #6: TO SHARE INFORMATION

This kind of argument involves an exchange of information with each party, in hopes that the other side sees the folly of his ways and reaches a level of enlightenment that resolves the argument. Sadly, it rarely works out that way, and talking by itself doesn't quite eradicate the problem.

Here's an example: Fourteen-year-old Emily asked for permission to sleep over at a girlfriend's house. Emily's mom confirmed the invitation in a phone call to the friend's mother and agreed to the sleepover. What Emily hadn't told her mom was that they were also going to a party at a boy's house, which her mother only learned about by overhearing her daughter's conversation when she dropped her off. Upset over having been deceived, Emily's mother promptly cancelled the sleepover, and an argument naturally ensued.

To their credit, they handled the situation calmly. Each described what they had done and why. Emily explained she was afraid her mother wouldn't have approved of the party, and sensing this, she said she had planned to ask her mom for permission just before they left. Her mother described her disappointment over her daughter's apparent sneakiness. Each left feeling they had a better understanding of why the other acted as they did, and it might seem as if they had taken care of business pretty effectively. They did—almost.

What they failed to do was to make a plan for the future, such as how Emily should handle it next time, discuss why deception leads to lack of trust and what the consequences would be if this ever happened again. Although they accomplished much in sharing information, they didn't take care of the whole issue. It's a great start, but if it's not complete, you run the risk of a repeated situation that could become far more explosive next time. Sharing only information leaves each party feeling pretty good, as if they really accomplished something. Indeed they have, but the satisfaction is for a job half done. I liken it to laying out all of the ingredients for a meal on the counter then just looking at them. Without the work, nothing is going to change.

In this case, Emily may sneak off to a future party, justifying her action with, "I thought you said it was okay as long as I didn't lie about it." Or she might be surprised when she finds herself grounded for a month, complaining, "You never told me you were going to ground me. Last time we just talked about it." And the mother may assume her daughter clearly understood what was expected and the consequences if she broke the rule. However, their heart-to-heart talk omitted explaining just what the rule would be from that point on. So if you and your child fight to get your points across, consider yourself on the right road, but not yet at your final destination.

GOAL #7: TO SOLVE THE PROBLEM

Whereas most arguments are unproductive, counterproductive, or downright destructive, some are truly attempts to arrive at workable solutions to genuine problems. When problem-solving is truly the motivation for an angry encounter, there's hope for a positive outcome.

When you focus on the solution, it's much harder to get side-tracked by manipulation and personal attacks that angry children throw at you. And if the child learns over time you're committed to working out a fair solution, he'll grow to trust you. If he senses you only want to win, or you don't follow through on promises for discussion, he won't trust you. Under that circumstance, he may think angry attacks are his only chance to get his way.

Pursuing this goal of solving the problem will take a good deal of work. Use it right, and the result is a child feeling he was listened to and that you're both modeling a more thoughtful approach to conflict. Remember that angry children have ineffective problem-solving skills and will readily resort to attack mode. This is your chance to teach how to problem-solve. Arguments don't have to lead to more tension and anger. View them as opportunities to work with your child to come up with answers that you can both live with. As he learns to use effective problem-solving, he will learn he does not have to resort to threats and fighting. Healthy self-esteem goes up and the arguments go down.

Ten Steps to Problem-Solving

Especially in the heat of anger, our problem-solving skills may desert us, and angry children lack these skills, even in the best of times. Work through these steps together and see how much more readily your child lives with the answers you give:

1. *Keep your focus.* Recognize that what seems like a solvable problem may not seem that way to the angry child. When people argue, emotions cloud thinking, and the focus shifts from problem resolution to attack. Calm down, take a deep breath, and put the focus back on the actual problem, not the attack it has provoked.

2. *Get details.* Identify just what you're arguing about. Sometimes each side has the facts so confused that listening sets you back on the track to resolution.

3. *Name your goals.* What will this look like when it's finished? Go beyond determining a winner and look to the long-term. Your child's

immediate goal may be to stay out late. Your goal may be to establish trust so you don't have to worry whenever he is out. He may be less interested in your long-term goal, but an older child will recognize that both goals can be merged into one if you agree that he can use tonight as a means of showing he can be trusted.

4. *Brainstorm solutions.* There's more than one route to every destination. By brainstorming, you may be surprised what pops up. During this stage it's important that you don't criticize any of your child's suggestions; otherwise you may fight over ideas before they have a chance to take shape. Generate many ideas and list them all for now.

5. *Evaluate these ideas.* Go over each one carefully. Weigh its merits. Drop the impossible ones and move forward with those that have potential. Will it get you to the goal you laid out? Work out the details from start to finish.

6. *Look for roadblocks.* Sometimes the best plan for one situation just won't work in another. Run the plan through in your mind. Ask each other to think of anything that could get in the way of making it work.

7. *Choose the plan you think will work the best.* Write it down if necessary. Make sure each side understands all the details.

8. *Put the plan into action.* Make sure there's a chance to test it, and allow plenty of time to see if it could work.

9. *Check it out.* Once you've had a chance to test the plan, go over it. If you fail to review its success or failure, it could lead to the next argument. Instead, ask, "Did it work?" And if it did, ask yourself why. Was it the plan or just luck? Your plan for teaching your child how to get his homework done without a hassle is hardly tested if the teacher gave none that night. Show your child humility and the willingness to try again if it didn't work.

10. *Change as needed.* If the solution works well, keep it. If it doesn't, modify it. If it was a dismal failure, drop it. This debriefing

and willingness to change is what makes for successful problem-solving. Remain flexible. Even a well-thought-out system can eventually fail if parent or child is unable to reevaluate it as the situation demands.

Nine Rules for Running a Family Meeting

When problems erupt, family meetings are an excellent way to deal with them. They should be open and honest discussions that focus on devising creative solutions or setting up new rules. Remember, they aren't trials, interrogations, or lectures. Here are some rules:

1. When a problem that can't readily be solved pops up, don't just talk about it, schedule a meeting to discuss it. The meeting should occur soon after you identify the problem, but *after* tempers have a chance to simmer down.
2. Everyone involved should be present, though some siblings may be excluded if it's a personal or potentially embarrassing subject. Otherwise it may be helpful for siblings to attend even if they're not directly involved, as they can learn problem-solving skills by watching.
3. Deal with one problem at a time. Someone defines the problem, and others get a chance to give their points of view.
4. Each person should get a chance to talk, without interruption, insult, and criticism. Turn off the TV and don't answer the phone.
5. Now, make the shift from haggling over the problem to reaching solutions. Agree on a set of goals that will achieve the ends you've mutually agreed upon.
6. Brainstorm a list of five or ten ideas to reach the goals. Don't discuss any of the individual ideas until your list is full.

7. Weigh the pros and cons of each. Get everyone's opinion.
8. Choose those that best reach the goals, and decide on steps for implementing them. Discuss how it will be handled if someone doesn't go along.
9. Once you've agreed upon a solution and decided how to get there, end the meeting with a feeling of accomplishment so everyone is willing to come back again to solve other problems another time.

Bad Argument Tactics

When you argue with an angry child, her lack of problem-solving skills may cause an escalation of the incident. Bad argument tactics like those that follow can completely derail or sidetrack a discussion and lead to further anger. It's the parent's job to recognize these unproductive argument patterns and tailor your responses accordingly. See if you or your child has ever resorted to any of these tactics:

- **The kitchen sink.** Everything, including the kitchen sink, has a part in this type of argument, and soon it's hard to tell what the real point is. You may have begun by commenting on dirty clothes on the floor, but suddenly you're arguing about homework, staying up late, choices of friends, and everything else that's happened over the past few years.

  If you see an argument is becoming all-inclusive, stop. It's best to settle one issue at a time. Resist the temptation to tackle everything at once. If another topic comes up, try saying, "I understand that's a concern, but we're not talking about that now. We can get to that later, after we've addressed this."

- **The poison pill.** When they sense an argument is not going their way, both children and adults may resort to the big guns, pulling out the one thing that stops the other cold in his tracks. Whatever is brought up is often a downright mean statement—even if it's true. "None of this would have happened if you didn't start seeing that guy when you were married to Dad" is an example of a poison pill that should be swallowed, not spoken in an argument. Similarly, "You're just like your father," or "You'll never amount to anything," can be painful to hear and linger for a child long after the subject of your fight is forgotten. Never lob one of these at your child, and if he tosses a poison pill, understand that he may be sidetracking you, or lashing out to cover his fear that he's losing control of the argument. Stay focused on the issue. If tempers are too high, take a break and try again later.

- **Déjà vu all over again.** Just when you think an issue has finally been settled once and for all, back it comes again. Your child may simply be venting old pain from a former event. Determine the cause. If it's indeed unresolved, resolve it. Realize that some wounds take a long time to heal. Or your child may not understand the situation in the same way you do. Make sure you both understand each other, and see it through to the end.

- **Mirror-mirror.** When the queen in Snow White asked, "Who's the fairest of them all?" she didn't like the answer she got—and neither will your child. If you compare him in the heat of an argument with, "Why can't you be more like Bobby down the street?" your child may feel inadequate. Just as comments like "The other parents are so cool, why can't you be like them?" are hurtful to you, your child will resent being held to another child's standard. Praise your child for who he is, but help him work to become all he can be, not a carbon copy of someone else. The issue isn't acting like another, but doing the right thing.

- **The crystal ball.** When either party predicts what the other is going to say, you've got a crystal ball in the argument. Announcing, "I know what you're thinking," only shuts down communication without giving the other person a chance to respond honestly. Similarly, predicting the future with statements like, "I know you're going to fail so I'm not going to help you," hardly sets a goal worth working for. It's okay to point out the consequences life will dish out if your child continues along an errant path. But avoid making a prediction. Point out the choices they've made along the way, and help them to predict good and bad consequences of their actions. And if your child throws a crystal ball at you, sidestep it calmly and get back to the subject at hand.

- **The sky isn't blue.** Some children take a contrary position just to be difficult. I learned this from a young lady when I observed, "It seems like no matter what your parents say, you take the opposite position. I wonder if you'd argue with them about whether the sky is blue." To which she responded, "The sky *isn't* blue." If you're faced with such a contradictory child, she may try to show her own strength, or she may be at that preadolescent stage where kids see parents as weak. If the claim is absurd, try not to engage in a silly argument. Instead try spending positive time together. Get to know her. Is she somehow saying you view her as a baby? She might also want to show you she's got interests and ideas of her own. Urge her to express those rather than bickering over *your* thoughts and opinions.

- **Splitting.** This happens when a child sides Mom against Dad or one sibling against another. He may say, "Dad said I could if you say I can," when Dad merely said, "Ask your mother." He may get soft-hearted Mom to undo the punishment a tougher father put on him. With split families, a child learns that if you get one parent mad at the other, he just may get whatever he wanted as Dad tries to stick it to Mom. Be very, very careful whenever your child tells you negative things about the other. Listen, but be careful you don't give in to get back at the other parent.

- **You're imagining things.** Have you ever heard "That never happened" or "I didn't say that"? This tactic can make you a little crazy trying to remember what was said or done instead of focusing on the resolution. Similarly, your child may attempt to dismiss the significance of the event with "No big deal," "Who cares?" or "So what?" If it happened, it happened. Act on the facts, or at least on your best understanding of them. If your child lies to you, that may warrant additional consequences. And if you're suspicious about his involvement in something he shouldn't be doing, keep in mind that youth involved in drugs, alcohol, and illegal activities are likely to lie (that's why so many parents are surprised when they find out the facts from the police or a teacher). Follow your instincts and ask questions. It's your responsibility to investigate any sneaking around. Don't take "You're crazy, Mom" as an answer or a denial; see it for the evasion it is.

- **On strike.** When a child shuts down and refuses to do something, you'll hear declaratives like, "You can't make me." Responding with threats only worsens the situation. However, while it's literally true that you can't make her clean her room, consequences can motivate her to change her attitude. Don't throw out vague threats like, "You better or you'll be sorry"; let her clearly know the negative and positive consequences of her actions (or failure to act), such as "I cannot make you clean your room, but I can refuse to drive you to your friend's house until you do."

- **The martyr.** If you hear a child say, "I'll never amount to anything" or "I'm just stupid," he could be down on himself—or it could be a manipulative ploy to engage your sympathies. Look to see what's tied in with the martyr statement. Is he using it to get you to act the way he wants, or is it a genuine plea for help? You'll only know if you talk it over. If he says, "I couldn't clean out the garage because I had too much homework and you always yell at me if I don't get good grades," yet he was playing Nintendo an hour earlier, you're probably not getting the straight story. Kids may also play the martyr to get things they want, such as, "I don't have any friends because you won't buy me the clothes I want."

- **Whine, whine, whine.** Some kids have figured out that they can wear parents down over time. If they scream loud and long enough, they'll get what they want—even if you've already said no, and that's not a lesson you want to teach. If your child uses this tactic, try a progressive discipline. State your position firmly one last time and explain that you won't discuss it further. If they insist on whining anyway, they lose ten minutes more TV time for each time they bring it back up.

- **The brick wall.** Ever feel like you're talking to a brick wall? You're saying something, but your child ignores you. It can be infuriating. Make sure you haven't gone off on some overblown lecture. If you are simply venting, one can understand why your child might be ignoring you. Make your point clearly and move on. Check to see if your child is stewing over something and preoccupied. If so, put aside the argument temporarily if you can. But if it's just a tactic to get you mad, you may need to respond with a temporary grounding or have your child sit out a favorite activity until he decides to work it out with you.

Chapter Eight

Successful Discipline

YOU WOULDN'T be human if reprimanding your child didn't give you an occasional twinge. No matter how well-deserved the punishment is, your child is going to be a little miserable, and chances are you'll be unhappy too. It's natural for a parent to feel guilty or sad or uneasy when punishing children, because deep down we hate to deprive our kids of the things they want or cause them pain— even when the punishment is clearly warranted.

But it's doubly difficult with an angry child. Angry children see punishment as an attack: They blame you for administering the discipline and have a hard time understanding either your reasoning or the merits of the rules they broke. In response, they fight back. That's why it is so important to use effective discipline techniques with angry children. The way *you* handle the situation is another key ingredient that makes all the difference in the long run, even if the technique you try doesn't yield the desired results right away.

Who Is Your Model?

In my practice, I often ask parents to think about the best teacher they've ever had. What made that teacher so special and how did he or she handle discipline? I still think back to my high school geometry teacher. Every day he made it very clear to us what he expected us to learn, and if you got out of line, you faced the same rules and discipline whether you were the class clown or the valedictorian. And he expected success from everyone.

When someone did poorly on a test, they weren't simply punished with an F, but our teacher taught them to refuse to accept failure. We had to do the work over until we got it right. In addition he recognized that there was a time to work and a time to play, and often found a way to mix the two together to make learning fun.

He was and continues to be a great role model for me. Who is yours? Is it an individual, or maybe a few traits from several different people? Try to emulate these models as you parent, not the person you saw an hour earlier in the grocery checkout line, shouting at his child.

Discipline Without Anger

Your first goal as a parent in disciplining without anger is to take control without being controlling. Children need and want to know what the rules are even if they rebel against them. And an effective parent cannot shy away from the job. Consistently enforced and fair rules give children a sense of security and predictability in their world. Discipline need not be oppressive; you can bring control to the house while still giving your child plenty of latitude to make decisions, explore, and grow.

A controlling parent, on the other hand, tries to prevent bad behavior by being a dictator who rules every aspect of a child's life. Trust plays no part in the equation for these parents who feel they must be authoritarian lest their child step over the line. Any child, especially an angry child, will rebel against the overcontrolling parent. In turn, a volatile situation will escalate even further as the parent tries to find even sterner punishments, and the child tries to find ways around them.

Rather than get caught in the battle of who has the most power, take a step back. There may be times when you have to ask her to do something "Because I said so," but this probably isn't the time. Over the years, I've been impressed by the way many families have learned to think through difficulties and help their children. So if there is no logical reason why he cannot finish his basketball game with his friends before he cleans his room, you may be better off working through the challenge of how to build responsibility over time than going for instant compliance. On the other hand, if you told him he had to clean his room before he went outside because guests were coming over, that's a different story. In this case, if you want his ignoring your requests to stop, you'll probably need to punish him. Behaviors you want to see less of, as we'll discover, require negative discipline.

Similarly, if your daughter has told you she does not like cauliflower, and you put it on her plate anyway, you'll both be a lot happier if you don't turn this situation into a power struggle. Trying to bend your child's will to yours over something that's ultimately unimportant may unnecessarily make *you* feel angry, frustrated, guilty, and defeated, and create a conflict where none existed previously.

Over the years, I've also learned (sometimes the hard way) that letting my daughter make decisions for herself had a far greater impact than having me keep control. If she wanted to purchase a toy or some clothing with her own money, even if it was overpriced or of poor quality, we would discuss it, and then go with her decision. Later, when she saw it on sale, or her toy broke, she lived with the results. Those provided a far more valuable lesson than arguing with her in the store ever would have accomplished.

The first goal of discipline is to stay calm. When we lose control of our emotions, we lose control of our actions as well. That's when we parents can end up doing things we later regret. We may hand out absurd punishments or threats, speak to our kids in belittling ways, or maybe even lash out physically—all of which only worsen the situation. The angry child who struggles to understand both his own feelings and yours is all too likely to view your reaction as a threat and strike back.

Unless your child is in imminent danger, take some time to think through the problem before issuing your verdict. Then come back to attack the problem, not the child.

Discipline is a method of teaching your child to develop into a better person, but remember that the final exam day is a long way off. To continue the metaphor, life is filled with little quizzes that will test both of you, and you will have time to make changes after each one. Children flourish when you take the time to show them the right way to do things, expect only what they are able to do at their level, and patiently nurture them to learn more along the way. They'll make mistakes. They'll challenge you. But keep foremost in your mind that you are on a long road of learning.

Start small. If you are up to your neck in problems, there is little to be gained from choosing the biggest, toughest problems first. An angry child will likely fight your attempts to get control. But by starting with little issues and taking small steps, you build confidence and she will learn to trust you to handle the situation effectively and fairly. From those little steps, you will build big cooperation.

Five C's of Commonsense Parenting

When you discipline, make sure the techniques you use are fair, simple, and effective. After working with families for years, I've developed an approach that can be adapted to many situations. The cornerstone of this approach is what I call the five C's: Choices, Clarity, Consequences, Communication, and Consistency. By keeping these five elements foremost in your mind when the need to discipline arises, you can keep the problems that contribute to anger to a minimum—and get better, more productive results. Let's look at each.

CHOICES

People see situations according to what's important to them, and react based upon their own personal goals and beliefs. As parents, we see something and must choose whether to act, knowing that we can't deal with everything, and pick our battles.

How you define the problem contributes to the number and types of options you have. Dividing your child's behavior into categories— those you'd like to see more of (the new good behaviors), those you want to see less of (the bad behaviors), and those you want to see stay the same—provides a helpful basis upon which to make choices. Usually those behaviors causing the most grief demand the biggest reaction from parents. It's just as important, however, for a parent to direct energy into making desirable behaviors occur more frequently. Whether a behavior is defined as one a parent wants to see "less often" (such as "stop leaving your dirty dishes on the table") or "more often" (such as "put your dirty dishes in the sink") could be different strategies to change the same behavior problem.

The third area, behavior you want to see stay the same, is important as well. No matter how bad it all seems, there is bound to be something your child is doing that is okay or even good. Even when there is turmoil in the home, it's comforting for a child to realize that some of her behavior is acceptable. Too much criticism will tear down a child's confidence and weaken her desire to cooperate. (Remember that children need teachers and models more than they need critics.)

When a child gets the message that his or her parent likes something about them, cooperation becomes more likely. It also boosts a parent's confidence to know success with their child is possible despite all the problems. This is particularly important for families of angry children who otherwise focus too much on the negative.

Remember that in the midst of chaos there are many things about your child that you love and want to continue. While trying to bring about change in certain behaviors, you'll want to nurture the continuance of others.

From these three areas parents will make choices for action. Making the right choices can be challenging. A misunderstood situation, or parenting beliefs that lead to trouble, will also lead to problems in making the right choices.

Exercise: What to Change, How to Change

Get out a piece of paper and make three columns: (1) What you want your child to do more often; (2) What you want to happen less often; (3) What you want to stay the same. Now brainstorm for a while and write down actions for your child under each category. Don't worry about getting all the details down yet. We will work on that later.

Usually, parents whose child is a handful can fill a page with lots of behaviors they want to see go away. Occasionally parents find the "Stay the same" category difficult, especially when they've been experiencing problems. Know that your child is *always* doing *something* that is okay. If you're having trouble coming up with things for the "More of" category, take some of the "Less of" items and look at their opposite. For example, "No lying" would be listed as "Tell the truth more often." Phrasing in the positive increases your success rate and sets a goal. Here's an example of what one mother came up with for her eight-year-old:

More of:

· Keep room clean and put toys away
· Tell the truth and show respect
· Study hard and do homework right after school

- Treat her friends nicely and share her toys
- Follow rules in games
- Stay away from things that are not hers

Less of:

- Lying, backtalk, and whining
- Picking on her sister
- Interrupting when mom is on the phone
- Putting up a fuss about going to bed
- Cheating in games
- Leaving a mess in the kitchen
- Criticizing everyone and having a negative attitude

Stay the same:

- Is kind when she wants to be
- Is nice to her cat and affectionate with people
- Treats her grandparents well
- Eats all the food on her plate
- Doesn't do dangerous things
- Writes neatly and dresses nicely
- Plays well with her baby brother for short periods

Notice how this parent came up with several things she hoped would remain the same. These stay-the-same behaviors give a parent a reason to compliment his or her child when everything else seems to be going wrong, which gives you *both* reason to be optimistic and stave off discouragement.

Once you have your categories, the next step is to make decisions about what you'll work on first. Try to avoid the whims of the moment or just those issues that cause the most conflict. If you tackle too many thorny problems at once, you might give up too soon. Instead, base your choices on the behaviors most likely to change. Then rank them according to the following factors:

■ What you're *able* to work on. You'll never be able to break a teen's dependence on the phone entirely, nor can you enforce it 24/7 if you try, so avoid the impossible. You must have the ability to make the change happen. Do you expect your child to earn an A in math when it has always been her worst subject? If so, you may need outside help, such as a tutor, to achieve the goal.

■ What you're truly *willing* to work on right now. Sometimes we make choices based upon another's complaints or advice. A relative or friend may feel your child needs to dress more conservatively, while you're willing to tolerate ripped jeans and blue hair if the trash is taken out. If your own heart is not into the change, don't start with that item, but move it down the list. You can tackle it later once you build a record of success and trust.

■ What's *developmentally appropriate.* Certain behaviors are typical of certain ages. When the expectations are mismatched with the child's abilities, it's difficult, if not impossible, to win cooperation. A two-year-old will have trouble eating with a fork. A six-year-old may not make perfectly formed letters. School-age children may need help recalling household rules. When a teenager wants to spend time with friends instead of family, that may be an adjustment the family needs to work out with their teen rather than expect the child to do all the changing.

■ What your *child is willing to do.* Changing a behavior that's very dear to your child may not be the place to start if you are hoping to build on success. Suddenly taking a favorite blanket away from a five-year-old, or telling a lonely fourteen-year-old he can no longer associate with a certain friend, may cause new problems. By choosing something on which you can readily get cooperation and effect change with a reasonable amount of effort, you give your child the opportunity to build a pattern of success—and yourself too. This doesn't mean you let your child be in charge of what goes and what stays. Parents can still have those dearly held behaviors high on their priority list. Again, it's a question of starting off on the right foot and working from success to success.

CLARITY

Once you've made initial decisions about where to start, translate your choices into clear goals that everyone can understand. "Improve your attitude" or "study harder" are all well and good, but how does a child (much less the parent) measure the child's progress? Clarifying involves knowing the who, what, and when of a child's behavior, which in turn may even reveal some of the why. Often, when you learn the causes of poor behavior, you can prevent it from recurring.

The Who, What, When, and Why of Clarifying

Bad behaviors—and the solution to them—don't occur in a vacuum. The *who* part of clarifying means identifying the other individuals, and that may include caregivers, the child, or friends who may be an accomplice to the problem, as well as its solution.

How does your child act around different caregivers? Does she lose control with one but remain happy with another? Does she behave better around Mom than Dad? Try to break this down person by person and see what you can learn. Ask the other adults why they think your child has more or fewer problems around them. Are they more demanding? Maybe they make it a point to have more fun, and are less stringent regarding rules. Perhaps they just have different standards than you.

Ask yourself also why this particular behavior you've targeted is a problem for you. Do other people think it's bad? Is there something that makes you supersensitive to it? If it's your issue, solving it will involve changing your attitudes about the issue. Knowing that you play a role can come as a great relief, since you can then play an active role in the solution.

It's also essential to find out if someone else is involved in *making* the trouble happen. It could be one of your child's friends, even another parent trying to prove a point. Analyze who the accomplice is, how they're contributing to the situation, and how their influence can be neutralized. Knowing the accomplices will tell you who else you need to talk to, discipline, or just plain keep your child away from.

Who

A major part of understanding *who* is involved means you need to understand your child's temperament, and developmental level. Temperament is your child's individual style of handling the world. A child with a positive mood, good attention span, one who is not too impulsive or too intense, is easy to handle. On the other hand, children with a high activity level, short attention span, short fuse, and impulsive/easily distracted nature can require every parenting skill and ounce of energy you can muster. These children need even more structure, reminders, and plenty of clarity in your rules. Fortunately, most children fit in between the two extremes, and by knowing your child's temperament, you can adjust your rules and expectations accordingly. A child who takes time to adapt to new situations may need more time to get used to things, so support would go a long way before rushing her into new things. Planning a four-hour museum visit for a child with a short attention span is a setup for frustration that could be prevented with properly aligned expectations.

Whereas temperament describes what is unique to your child, developmental stages tell us what is common at different ages. The younger a child is (preschooler, for instance), the more they see the world revolving around them, and the more difficult it is for them to understand another's point of view. Rules are black and white to them, and they rarely understand why you are allowed to do something they are not.

As kids progress through school, their thinking expands, yet they're still not able to reason as an adult. The school-age child grows in her ability to understand how she would feel if others treated her the way she treats them. Because school-age kids no longer think in all-or-nothing terms, they may try hard to find exceptions to rules and test out the gray areas.

As kids move toward adolescence, the opinions of friends surpass parental judgment, and so does spending time with their peers. Some mature teens have a great capacity to do the right thing despite what peers may pressure them to do, while others, with less self-esteem, can be more susceptible to peer pressure.

Teens are better able to apply reasoning and logic to the choices they make and their consequences, but keep in mind that their skills are still limited. Complicating this even more is the emotional volatility that accompanies hormonal maturation. Lengthy passionate arguments may ensue, with teens sometimes arguing down absurd paths and jumping from subject to subject. Despite these hurdles, teens can be quite caring and generally desire better relationships, with parents and other authority figures. They don't look for fights, but when the fights come, they hold on to the hope that a better relationship with Mom and Dad is not impossible.

So when you clarify, keep your child's age and stage in mind. The issue may have less to do with a struggle involving you, and everything to do with a child's maturation.

What

The *what* aspect is the most important part of clarifying. Use words that describe exactly what happens, behavior you want to change, not a concept like "He has an attitude." You can work on behaviors, not on concepts. For instance, I remember the mother in my office complaining about her son. "He's bad," she said. And when I asked for a little more elaboration, she just said, "You know, *bad*." I asked again. She said, "He's bad in the morning, bad in the afternoon, and bad the whole damn day." I could tell she was fed up, but I had no idea what the boy was actually doing, since labels mean different things to different people. Thus, when you clarify your choices, replace vague descriptions with precise thoughts. Give concrete examples. That mother had more to work with when she could list examples like: He forgets to feed the dog, and he won't put his dirty clothes away.

When

The *when* refers to problems that may occur at certain times or on certain days. Do the problems seem associated with any events in particular? We can find clues to the causes if we pay attention to things that precede or follow the misbehavior. Is he more angry in the morning or evening? Are weekends different from school days? Is she grouchier just before tests at school?

On another level, knowing when the trouble starts may give us all the information we need to take action. One family noticed a lot of bickering before dinner. The mother had the kids wait to eat until dinnertime so they didn't leave food on their plates. When she experimented with allowing light snacks about an hour before dinner, the family found the squabbles diminished greatly.

In the case of divorced families, kids can understandably have trouble making a quick emotional transition from one parent's house to the other's. Different rules, different homes, different neighborhoods, different friends. And they have to let go of one parent and connect with the other. They may even worry that if they have too good a time at one house, it may upset the other parent, or it can leave the child feeling guilty if he's too happy. That's a lot of adjustments to make, even if the child seems used to it. It's not surprising that many families find that first hour or two after a handover potentially tense. The lesson here is to avoid pressures the first thing in the door.

Why

With the *why*, we're trying to determine the motivation behind a child's behavior. Be aware that this question doesn't always lead to fruitful insights. I point this out since parents can get themselves unnecessarily worked up trying to discern all the reasons a child acts the way he does; sometimes you simply won't have a clue. If you struggle to find all the meaning behind a behavior, you may never act.

Have you ever demanded of your child to explain why she acted a certain way or broke a particular rule, only to be told, "I don't know"? You probably got a little miffed, and the situation may have worsened. But occasionally "I don't know" is a truthful response. Kids simply do things without thinking, and often it's not done with malice. They may be acting out of habit, nothing more. Furthermore, for some behaviors, like constantly cluttering the stairs with dirty clothes or slapping his sister, it's not critical to know the motive. You can still punish the act.

When it *is* important to know the *why*, find out. If the child's act was warranted (which *you* need to judge) it's usually right on the surface. But sometimes the causes lie deeper. Perhaps there are problems at school or home. Here, knowing the *why* tells you that you must address the causes if you're to help your child behave the way you want him to and keep the peace. Sometimes, angry rebellion is also a cry for help. A certain amount of structure in the home can be a way of showing you care enough about your child to make sure he behaves. Ask yourself: Is there something behind the persistent misbehavior? If that something requires action or help, *take care of it.*

CONSEQUENCES

Discipline is an educational process. To make the most of it, you need to control the outcome of a child's good or bad actions. Directing your child toward outcomes that reinforce good behaviors and diminish the frequency of less desirable ones is an obvious goal. But ideally, any punishment you dole out should also be a learning experience. It should be aimed at helping the child, not just venting your anger, and it should fit the age/developmental level of your child. Avoid choosing a particular punishment or reward just because it was how you were (or were not) raised.

Many books have been written on discipline, and even experts differ over which approach is best. But there are techniques I've found most valuable in defusing the anger that often arises from discipline. Because different disciplinary techniques are right for different age groups, I've grouped them by age level. Remember, behaviors you want to see more of or want to stay the same will best be handled with positive discipline or rewards. Behaviors you want to see less often are best handled with negative discipline or punishment.

Preschool

Praise. Preschoolers respond very well to praise. Make sure to be complimentary when you see her act the "right" way. Praise her for using good manners, sharing, taking turns, being patient, and trying hard without losing her temper. For young children, it's important to praise at the moment; if you wait until later, she may not understand what you are talking about. However, you can bring it up later as a reminder of how proud you were to see her good behavior.

Teaching the right way. Young children still have a lot of learning to do, and they often learn best through example. If he gets frustrated while trying to assemble a puzzle, suggest how to try another way. But also make sure you send the message to "relax" and "stay calm." And remember that your behavior serves as a model. Young children are especially adept at following your lead. They look upon adults with admiration and will watch how you behave. Whether you put away your things or leave a mess, treat family members with respect or insult them, and stay calm or lash out in anger, are likely to influence how they approach these same issues.

Time-out. This is a common punishment for preschool-age children. To make a time-out work best, remind your child ahead of time what the forbidden behavior is and what will happen if she does it. You may even have a brief practice session. Place a chair in the corner or away from fun things like TV or toys. Use a kitchen timer with an alarm (so you don't forget when the punishment is over and leave her there too long). Usually one minute of time-out for each year of age is sufficient. If she gets up and leaves before the time-out is over, add another minute. Once the agreed-upon time has passed, briefly remind her of the rule and what will happen if she breaks it again. Give her a word of encouragement and send her on her way. If she breaks the rule again, it's back to time-out.

Parents should avoid adding to the anger by increasing the time-outs unreasonably. Most children need a few rounds before they learn the lesson or learn you mean business. Be patient.

Chill-out. This technique for preschoolers isn't quite a punishment, or a reward, but it can be an effective strategy for keeping a volatile situation under control. Use the chilling-out method during the buildup or spark stages, when you see emotions bubbling up and the child's temper reaching the boiling point. You may want to enforce a chill-out even if he has not yet broken a rule but you see the inevitable on its way (as when a four-year-old trying to play cars has them taken away repeatedly by a younger sibling). Distract him and ask him in simple terms how to handle the situation he's getting into. Maybe add some humor, and suggest alternatives, such as sharing. You may also need to remind him of the rules. All of this may be the only intervention he needs.

Checklists. The reward system works with preschoolers as long as it's kept very simple, especially for behaviors you want to see more of.

Make up a chart and post it someplace like the refrigerator door or her bedroom wall. Define the targeted behavior in simple terms, such as: Take a bath when asked, eat with a fork rather than with hands, go to bed calmly. Each time she does what's asked, she gets a check (star, sticker, whatever) on the chart. Praise her each time she earns one. If you want, she can earn a small toy or a special privilege (such as a trip to the ice cream store) when she reaches a predetermined goal. But make sure the reward is something you can follow through on fairly quickly; if you put off rewards too long, the checklist loses its effectiveness.

School-age children

Sit-out. Sitting out means missing a favorite activity. It can be a logical consequence (such as not getting a video because last time he put up a fight at the video store). Whereas consequences need to be more immediate with preschoolers, you can delay the action slightly with school-age children.

Chores. Assigning household tasks as a consequence of poor behavior is as old as time, but it's still a useful technique, even with an angry child. In many cases the consequence could logically fit the behavior. Does she leave dirty dishes out? She must help to wash all the dishes. Did he walk across the floor with muddy boots? Vacuum the rug. Did she play in her brother's room and leave his toys out? Then she needs to clean her brother's room before she can go out to play. If the child refuses, she should be made to sit out other activities until she comes around.

Writing. This can be used as an effective learning tool for school-age children. Some parents have their child write an essay about what happened and how to handle the situation better next time. Some have the child write a sentence such as "I will treat my family with respect" ten or twenty times. Another family might have their child copy a brief Bible passage that taught a positive message.

Natural consequences. Sometimes the most effective thing to do is . . . nothing. When the child's inaction leads to a natural consequence, it can be an effective learning tool. Perhaps he carelessly left a toy lie outside and the rain damaged it, or maybe he took too long doing a chore and missed his favorite TV show. Under these circumstances you may not have to do anything, since the natural outcome is a lesson in itself. My dad must have told me a hundred times to wear shoes outside. Once I stepped on a nail with my bare foot, he never had to remind me again.

Checklists. This more sophisticated version of what you tried with the preschooler focuses on one or more target behaviors at a time. Again, make sure you clearly define what the targets are, such as completing specific chores or going to bed on time. Each time the child complies, she'll earn a set number of points. Difficult tasks earn more points than easy ones. Let the child come up with a list of rewards to work toward, including some that require fewer points as well as bigger ones. The rewards can be privileges (like having a friend spend the night) or a coveted toy. Do not, however, agree to rewards that aren't appropriate for the child's age or that conflict with your family values, such as violent video games. Sometimes a child will come up with a truly gargantuan reward. If you see fit to keep it on the list, assign it an appropriate value, as did the parents of a nine-year-old who wanted a Corvette and assigned it a value of 200,000 points.

Whatever is chosen, make sure to select some items that he can eventually learn from. A reward that will take months to earn may be of little value if your child doesn't have the stamina to stay with the task. Also, once the child has earned the points, don't take them away, as you may find she quickly gives up. Don't demand perfection either. The value of a checklist is that the child can earn points over time even if she occasionally makes mistakes. On the other hand, don't give the reward unless she has earned it. A child will not be motivated to save up points for a trip to the movies if the family regularly goes to the movies anyway. The rewards should be something special, just a few items at a time. A long checklist may be too overwhelming to anyone, especially a child.

Adolescents and teenagers

Grounding. This takes away your child's freedom of movement for a set period of time. Make the time period significant enough to be effective but not absurd. Make the time fit the crime. One night or one week may be warranted, depending upon the rule that was broken or the severity of the behavior being punished. Stop and think before shouting out an unrealistic punishment in frustration and anger. Grounding a child for a long time period may leave you without any discipline options. A father of teenage girls who stayed out past curfew in September grounded them for the rest of the school year. The result? When the girls misbehaved, they would say, "What are you going to do now?" Their father was backed into a corner with nowhere else to go. And be prudent about grounding during events that are very important to your child, such as the prom or big game. Overly harsh punishment focuses your child's attention on the unfairness of your reprisal rather than the infraction that brought it on.

Fines. For repeated behavior such as swearing, hitting, slamming doors, leaving food out after he made a midnight snack, a monetary fine may be a useful consequence if your child has money from an allowance or part-time job. Fining works best when specific behaviors have specific costs. If chores don't get done, rather than take away the entire allowance, prorate it and withhold a portion for each day the chores went undone. That way when your child sees the money he could have earned, the loss is a little more apparent. And while you shouldn't be hard, especially on younger kids, do assign values to these behaviors that will make a point to your child. A fourteen-year-old who loses twenty-five cents for not taking out the trash may figure it worth a quarter to let Dad do it instead.

Community service. Many families and schools actively encourage kids to give time to their communities to teach responsibility. It can also be a very effective way to demonstrate the consequences of bad behavior. To help deal with his sons riding their bikes through the neighbor's yard, a dad had his sons rake the leaves or mow the grass in the neighbor's yard to learn respect for their property. Another family had their children take trash bags and help clean up a street in their community as a lesson to stop littering.

For any age

Progressive discipline. For habitual behaviors, it's appropriate to escalate discipline each time it recurs. For example, the first time a youngster grabs the toy from her sister, you could use a time-out. But let her know that each time she does this again, you may add a minute to her time-out.

With an older child, the period of grounding may last longer with each infraction (for each fifteen minutes he comes home after curfew, there will be a day of grounding). This teaches the child that as the behavior gets worse, so does the punishment.

Catch good behavior. Children crave praise from parents, and too often we focus only on their bad behavior. When we pay attention to their good behavior, it can have a remarkable effect on their actions. In fact, some children start fights because they're bored or want attention. By catching her being pleasant, you give that attention. Children respond much better if they learn that Mom and Dad are noticing their brighter moments as well as their less laudable ones.

Exercise. This may bring to mind Marine boot camp, but requiring some physical exertion from your acting-out child has multiple benefits. One mother who exercised each day by walking a mile would have her ten-year-old accompany her whenever he was getting a little too ornery. This was particularly beneficial to him, as he exercised very little and was overweight, and it gave them some positive time together. Consider assigning a lap or two around the school track or a walk around the block.

Practice, practice. Does your child come in the house and throw his coat on the floor? Practice coming back in the house and hanging it up. Is her backpack such a mess that she can never find her homework? Have her clean it out each night and practice putting things away neatly. Yes, old habits can be hard to break. You may need to go through the same behavior a few times each night to erase the old habit and imprint the new one, but stick with it. Walking your child through the correct behavior shows her that you care about the behavior, not about oppressing her pointlessly.

COMMUNICATION

If you are trying to instill a new behavior or banish an old one on a permanent basis, you must communicate with your child's other caregivers and teachers so you're all on the same page. When it comes to parenting, many of us expect our children to know what we want, what we expect, and what's not acceptable, without our telling them.

You have to let children know what you expect, what the rules are—and what the consequences are of breaking those rules. And you may have to *keep* telling them. Children, especially youngsters, have an uncanny ability to forget. When introducing a new rule, it's wise to ask your child to repeat what you just said to ensure he understands the message as you said it, not as he thinks he heard it. A good communication will include a request, a reason, then a reminder, and a response to your child's action. Keep these elements in mind as you go over house rules.

Another very important part of communication is to make sure you are instilling positive lessons in your child's life as well as discipline. If you focus only on punishment, your child may avoid the proscribed behaviors out of fear, but won't develop the sort of internal morals that will carry him through in the future. Make sure your child knows you love him. Don't simply assume he does; tell him you love him, in no uncertain terms. Spend time together too, for actions are the best proof.

Teach him your values for how people should be treated. Listen to what he thinks and what he understands about your lessons. The messages you teach will be what he takes with him long after he's moved out of your sight or out of your home. Take the time to communicate. If you did a good job clarifying your desires and defining the consequences, your communication will be much easier.

The Four R's of Communicating Discipline

First R. When you want a child to do something, make a *request.* Ask your child in a way that you would also appreciate being asked. This is a form of the Golden Rule. Start off by sending a message that you expect cooperation. You're also modeling how to talk with respect.

Second R. Give a *reason* if necessary. Reasons are needed when it's a new rule, a change in plans, or a reminder about the rewards or consequences of not getting the job done. Note that giving reasons every time is not always necessary if the child already knows the rules.

Third R. If your child has not cooperated within a reasonable amount of time, *remind.* Everyone deserves a reminder when distracted by another activity. Ask your child to look at you or to repeat what you asked as a means of making sure he or she heard you.

Fourth R. Finally, *respond.* If the child is cooperating with your request, offer a kind word or a pat on the back. If you still don't have the cooperation, now use an appropriate discipline. A dozen reminders don't teach the child to listen and may only set you up for anger.

CONSISTENCY

With any approach to discipline, your efforts will go to waste if you fail to remain consistent. Communication with other caregivers fosters consistency. So does your own resolve not to allow your child to get away with misbehavior just because you're too tired to discipline or not strong enough to enforce your choices and the consequences.

In our fast-paced lives, refusing to make exceptions for the sake of convenience can be very hard indeed. But without some level of consistency, your child will get mixed messages about what is right and wrong. That will make them less accepting of the consequences when you *do* have time to enforce them, and result in justifiable anger. When you have made specific choices about what won't be allowed, clarified them, defined the consequences and communicated these, it's much easier to be consistent. If you find your child's behavior isn't changing, ask yourself if you're really sticking with the program. If you aren't, you can hardly blame your child.

Remember, nothing works if you don't try it, and things rarely last if you don't follow through. Stick with your program, even if there are rough spots. Talk it over and get advice, if needed. But if your goal is to help your child change for the better, you'll need to hang in there long enough to see change. If things don't improve, you may have to go back to one of the earlier steps (Choices or Clarification) and ask yourself if you're really focusing on the right target and if you have chosen workable goals.

Take notes and review them day by day to see if your methods are working. See if something different occurred that threw you off on a particular day. Reviewing your actions and results using the Five C's gives you an opportunity to check each step of the process to see what's working and what's not. But even with the best laid plans, if you fail to follow through, results will be mixed, at best. If you're having trouble with consistency, daily reviews of how you're doing help remind you to stick with your plan. And don't give up once you start to see success. Keep it up until the behavior you target is not just an occasional thing, but habitual.

Where to Get Help

• Parents Anonymous has many chapters nationwide where parents meet because their anger gets in the way of proper parenting and discipline. Some of these parents are truly afraid of their anger. Meeting in supportive settings with others, as well as with a trained facilitator, is free and of great benefit to these parents. Call 1-800-448-4906 to find a group near you.

• The National Committee for Prevention of Child Abuse also offers information for parents who feel their anger is running away with them, perhaps culminating in verbal, emotional, or physical abuse to their children. Call 312-663-3520 for more information.

• "Talking With Families About Discipline" is a booklet provided by Family Communications, the nonprofit organization that produces "Mister Rogers' Neighborhood." Send a business-size, self-addressed, stamped envelope to Family Communications Inc., 4802 Fifth Avenue, Pittsburgh, PA 15213, or call 412-687-2990.

• Local resources are prevalent in many cities to help parents through therapy, group counseling, literature, and other supports. Look under "Human Services" in your telephone directory, or call your local United Way office for referrals.

Chapter Nine

Winning the Daily Battles

I F YOU have an angry or out-of-sorts child, then you know the angst involved each day as you request cooperation from your son or daughter in simple tasks—everything from picking up toys, going to bed, setting the table, or doing homework. There are times it may seem that negotiating world peace is an easier prospect than gaining the teamwork it takes to function as a family should.

While most children might put up a minor fuss when asked to comply with a parent's request, remember from the ten traits of angry children discussed in Chapter 3 that these kids may automatically default into negative patterns and behaviors much more readily than their peers. Keep these traits in mind as you proceed in what may appear to be simple matters. Every parent's goal reading this chapter should be to gain cooperation rather than conflict, and while I won't go into great lengths in any one area, I hope that the suggestions I present will make your home much less of a battlefield and more the friendly retreat.

This chapter highlights common problems that could spark family meltdowns, including sibling rivalry, lying, picking up toys, tantrums in public places, and getting chores accomplished. I'll discuss the quitter, the late sleeper, the bedtime battle warrior, the whiner, the fussy eater, and the child who seems to move at a snail's pace. Swearing, allowances, homework, and teenage concerns have been added for older children as well.

Bad Habits and Dirty Dishes

Think back to the last time your child grabbed a snack. Did she clean up after herself or leave the dirty dishes on the table—or the floor or bed. You may have yelled, threatened, or pleaded with your child to clean up after herself, but it's the same old story—she doesn't listen, loses track of time, or otherwise isn't motivated to help. If your child is intentionally leaving a mess, perhaps in a passive-aggressive attempt to get back at you, that is a bad behavior that requires one kind of approach. Bad behavior can be corrected through discipline, which may motivate the child to change his or her ways.

Bad habits are another story. Kids, and adults, automatically continue habits without even thinking of the consequences. Many a child has developed the habit of walking away from a job without even thinking about it. It is frustrating to parents, and may seem like defiance, but arguing or punishment may not get you the results you want. Our minds operate much like a computer program. Once written, a program just repeats over and over until someone programs the computer differently. So, when a child has a bad habit, the answer lies in retraining, or reprogramming, his response to a particular situation.

In this dish dilemma, let your kids know that the next time they leave the dishes out, they can expect a lesson on cleaning up. Review the whole routine from bringing dishes to the kitchen, washing and rinsing them, drying and putting them away. With complete instructions, there will be no excuses of "I didn't know how" or "You never told me."

Next, have your child repeat the dish routine perhaps two to five times. Have him take a dish out of the cupboard and back to where he originally left it; he then carries it to the kitchen, washes it, dries it, puts it away, and so on. If the dirty dishes continue to accumulate, remind your child that practice makes perfect. Each time he forgets, the number of times he must run through the practice routine increases. This helps a child to reprogram his own mental computer.

Kids usually learn pretty quickly from this, but I've known children who pushed the number up to twenty times before they broke the old habit. Eventually they will surmise that it wastes longer periods of time just going through the motions. You can use this technique to help your child relearn any behavior you've gone over and over with him.

Sibling Battles

There will always be competition between siblings. Sometimes it's best to let brothers and sisters work out a situation, but at other times it's best for parents to step in and teach them how to handle it. Parents can act in one of five ways—as the coconspirator, the judge, the referee, the bystander, or the teacher.

The first and worst case is becoming a *coconspirator* with the children. A coconspirator says things like, "Well, you deserved it when she punched you" or suggests "Why don't you hit him back?" It doesn't help when a parent gangs up with one child against the other. No one wins, and the sibling situation usually worsens.

The second approach assumes the role of the *judge*. This is the best method when parents take the time to listen to all sides of the argument, let everyone have a turn, and then pass on a fair judgment and sentence. The judge controls the conversation, keeps people from interrupting one another, and makes sure she tracks down the facts. In the end, the judge's verdict stands. So when the kids have a fight, the judge brings the kids together for a hearing and goes through the whole procedure. Yes, it takes time, but that is the good news. The time you're spending listening to all sides of the story provides a great lesson in getting all the facts before someone jumps to a conclusion. It's also time during which kids cannot go back to playing, at least until the issue is settled. Finally, you can use it as a mechanism to get them calm. Children really like the idea of getting a chance to speak without interruptions from their sibling. If the situation gets heated, the judge calls for order, and then goes back to listening and questioning until all feel they have stated their case and been heard.

The *referee* has its place when the parent lacks the time to listen, or when the parent has witnessed kids breaking a rule. Under these circumstances, the penalty happens automatically. Again, it's important that parents act fairly. Just as a referee does not need to listen to long explanations, so too the parent can just take action. "I saw what you did and there is a rule about it. Period."

Being a *bystander* is a hands-off approach. When children already know very well what to do, there are times when it's best for parents not to get involved. Remind the children how to handle it, and let them work it out. But you still might use your judgment about whether you should act at the moment. Don't ignore a situation where you should get involved. If the kids are fighting, you may need to break it up. If they're deciding how to work out a problem, see what they can do. If they need help, step in. But when you can, give them a chance to apply the problem-solving strategies you've taught.

Finally, you can stem sibling rivalry in the role of *teacher*. Here, the responsibility still rests on the child, but with a catch. Children have to write down a description of the problem, and an idea or two on how to solve it. The parent, acting as teacher, can decide when the assignment is done correctly and if parts of it need to be rewritten before they go back to play. Writing a description of the problem encourages kids to carefully think through and be responsible for their solutions. It's more productive than just sending them to their rooms to sit, and the time they spend writing helps them calm down. If she uses a sarcastic approach, like writing "My brother is the problem and you should just get rid of him," do what a good teacher would do. The assignment isn't acceptable and needs to be reworked before it can be turned in. Make sure they follow through on the solutions. Any solution will take time, but with patience, siblings will get better at solving and preventing problems.

Lying

It's hard for any parent to believe that the sweet, totally open toddler or youngster they raised will ever be capable of any subterfuge or dishonesty. Indeed, many kids get away with fibs or worse for years before their parents get wise to them. Every parent faces a moment when he must question the truth of something his child has said, and while it may not feel good to harbor such suspicions, allowing a lie to go unchallenged doesn't do you *or* the child any good.

Angry kids tend to be especially prone to lying, as they will seldom accept responsibility for the bad things that happen around them. They may lie to get out of trouble, to get someone else in trouble, to get attention, to get something they want, or because they misunderstand the facts of some decision or situation. Some of these scenarios are serious, some innocent. Handling them wrong can spark unnecessary anger.

With such vivid imaginations, kids can't help but conjure up a few creative stories. Preschoolers who still have trouble distinguishing between real and pretend fall into this category. When a young child tells an imaginative tale, relabel it as a story—even compliment her on her impressive imagination. Older kids, however, will embellish a story as their imagination and memory start to influence one another (sort of like a child's version of a fish tale). When this happens, remind the child to stick to reality. You will have to use your judgment regarding how far you will let him stray from the facts. But let him know the value of truth in building trust. A child who is trusted will get a lot more respect from friends than the child who is known for telling tall tales.

Telling a lie is a different matter. A lie is a willful distortion of the truth. How you handle the situation when you catch your child in a lie depends on the motivation or purpose behind it:

- **Lies told to get out of trouble** boil down to variations on the theme, "I didn't do it." When you're certain a child is at fault, don't argue about whether he's lying; use appropriate discipline as a consequence for the forbidden deed. If he has also lied about it, there should be additional consequences for the deceit. Avoid bargains such as, "If you tell me the truth I won't punish you," since kids learn quickly that to tell a lie and then confess is a neat way to avoid any punishment. Instead say, "If you did something wrong there may be consequences, but if you lie on top of it, the consequences will be worse."

- **Lies told to get someone else in trouble** is a common tactic used by siblings to get back at one another. They report an alleged misdeed and stand smugly by as another is unfairly chastised or punished. This is a particularly difficult kind of deception to catch, as the untruth seems very plausible. Treat this as you would any other malicious act directed toward another. Let your child know that such lying won't be tolerated.

- **Lies told to get something** are a form of manipulation. Examples include, "I need the money to buy a birthday present for my friend," "Dad said it was fine with him if it's okay with you," "All kids listen to this CD . . . the lyrics are fine," or, "A couple of us are going to meet at my friend's house, it's not really a party and both of his parents will be there." In these cases you're better off checking out the story before making an accusation or handing down punishments. If you find out your child wasn't telling the truth, let him know you will no longer be able to take his claims at face value and will be checking out his stories from now on. That means it will take more time for him to get what he wants even when he does tell the truth, especially if the claim can't be immediately verified. That's the price to pay for violating your trust. And make sure that if he got something for his lie (like money or a toy), it's forfeited. Use your judgment as to when you start to take him at his word again in the future, but test his claims randomly for the sake of rebuilding trust.

- **Lies to get attention**, yarns about hitting home runs or meeting a famous person, are told by kids to impress friends and make up for poor self-esteem. But when the truth comes out, the friends will reject the fantasist. If your child makes up stories just to win friends, she needs your guidance and support. Punishment is generally not appropriate in these circumstances because the censure of peers is painful enough. What these children need is more understanding and help from you. Show her other ways to win friends' acceptance and build friendships.

Clean Up This Mess!

When you have children, you have toys—and often you have a mess as well. Picking their way through a minefield of discarded toys has caused many a parent to lose control and threaten to throw them all away if every last one isn't returned to its place—pronto. Rather than resulting in a tidy playroom, such tactics generally result in tears, lost tempers, and escalation of anger on both sides.

It's a little senseless to threaten to throw toys away. Save your voice and develop solutions for tidiness that will help your child maintain his toys, keep common areas clear, and ease family friction.

When toys are stuffed into one big box, it's a disaster waiting to happen. It seems the favorite toy is always the one on the bottom, which means he's made a mess before he's even started to play. Organization is the key. Sort toys into smaller bins and boxes, or onto shelves. If there are toys that never get played with, donate them to a charity where they will be appreciated, or suggest that your child have a toy sale to make money for something else he wants. Insist that whenever your child wants to play with a new toy, the old toy must be put back on the shelf first. Start teaching your child this procedure as early as age two or three.

When it's cleanup time, set a reasonable time limit. Sometimes a five-minute warning is helpful for young children to start winding down their play. You can even help clean up and make it into a game if you want, as long as that does not become the standard. If he tends to always walk away from his mess, it's time to take other action. One method is to give him the choice of who cleans it up. If he does it, great! But if he doesn't do the job within the stated time frame, get a bag and calmly start loading up the toys for storage. Keep the collected toys out of reach. If the cleanup goes more smoothly the next time, give lots of praise and allow your child to reclaim one toy from those you've quarantined. Each time he cleans up responsibly, he can select another toy from storage as a reward.

While it may take your child a while to catch on—here again, you're reprogramming an ingrained habit—sooner or later you won't be fighting over a mess. The trick is to stay calm, stick to the game plan, and resist belittling or nagging your child. And if you've stored away a toy that she never asks for again, pass it on. That's one less to pick up the next time.

Quitting

Angry children are easily frustrated and often lack the resources to tough out a situation that isn't going their way. Walking away can become a way of life if adults and other authority figures don't make the point that perseverance is a valuable commodity that brings its own rewards. How do you handle the child who begged to join the team, then wants to quit the first time the coach is critical of his play? How do you teach your child to honor his commitments, including promises to others or volunteer jobs? Try these approaches:

■ Help your child choose commitments wisely, such as jobs or sports involvement, according to his age and abilities. If his initial enthusiasm to go to practice turns to reluctance, explain that teammates and the coach are counting on him. Try to get him at least to complete the season, with the understanding that he need not sign up for another season. Focus on the improvements he's made, no matter how small, and set reasonable personal goals—"I will take more shots on goal," not "I will score a goal each game"—and notice when he achieves them.

■ Don't overload children or allow them to burden themselves with too many sports, baby-sitting jobs, church or community commitments. My coauthor told me of an instance where she was at first impressed with a young teenager's entrepreneurial spirit as she sent out flyers to be a baby-sitter. Loriann's enthusiasm quickly turned to frustration when this sitter never showed up. The girl's excuse was that she forgot she had previously committed to a party. After giving her one more chance at the responsibility, only to be left in another lurch, Loriann soon found a sitter who didn't take the job so cavalierly. The girl soon quit baby-sitting for other families as well, as she'd clearly overburdened herself.

■ Monitor your child's schedule and commitments by asking her what she's up to. Should you feel the schedule she's keeping doesn't allow for adequate study, play, or relaxation time, speak up and explain your concerns. But in the end, your child may have to learn the hard way. Unmet expectations or poor performance yields the same kind of repercussions for kids that they do in the adult world.

■ Look for other reasons why your child might want to quit or opt out of an activity. Is he being teased? Does she lack confidence? Does he lack the talent to be in the play, or is he just mad he didn't get the lead role? Does she need better equipment to play the sport well? Is he such a klutz that it's more embarrassing to continue? Be certain this isn't a "when the going gets tough, I go home" attitude.

Bedtime

Even the most tranquil domestic scenes can spiral out of control when it comes time to call it a night. Some children battle bedtime for hours. Not only do they become crankier as time passes, but so do the parents, who need both private time to relax or catch up on chores, as well as their *own* sleep. While it may be easier to let your child stay up that extra half hour than go to war just when everyone is most tired, it's vital that your child gets as much sleep as is age-appropriate. Kids who get enough sleep are generally happier than tired ones, and making sure your child is well rested is a good way to prevent many an angry outburst.

For a young child, institute a winding-down routine. Set a fair bedtime, and stick to it every night. Avoid any rough-and-tumble play late in the evening, and don't dispense sugary snacks near bed-time. Instead, have a quiet talk to review the questions of the day. Give him a warm bath, brush his teeth, read a quiet story together, and say good night. Make sure you put him in his bed; parents who get into the habit of allowing kids to sleep with them have an even harder time when they want their bed back to themselves.

At bedtime, keep the house quiet. A loud TV, talk, or laughter make kids feel they're missing out on things and attract the pitter-patter of little feet. One mother got into the habit of washing the dishes when her child went to bed; if he came out, she told him he could either help her with chores or go back to bed. One night he opted to help with the dishes. After that he chose sleep. Alternatively, you might use the time to read in bed, pay bills, or any other quiet pursuit.

It's not uncommon for children under age seven to be afraid of the dark. Never tease about the existence of monsters, because to children they are indeed very real. If your child persists in believing they lurk in the dark corners of her room, despite your best efforts to dispel the notion, enter her imagination. Use a spray bottle to spray an imaginary scent in the room that repels monsters. Encourage her to discuss ways she could trick the monsters into leaving her alone. Homemade signs might keep monsters away. And prayers can give your child courage to deal with fears.

On nights when he has a bad dream, take a few moments to reassure him that all is well. Otherwise, observe the rule that after bedtime, kids stay in bed without exception. No snacks, no more stories. Even conversation can be reason to fight off sleep, so no more talking. If he gets up, quietly escort him back. Be gentle and understanding but firm. And if he sneaks into your bed during the night, you'll be better off getting up and putting him back in his bed, no matter how tired you are.

The added perk of getting to bed on time is not only a better-rested family, but having enough time in the morning to prepare for work or school at a leisurely pace. (Remember the frantic family? Well, this solution helps on that count also.)

Older children, especially teens, often do not get enough sleep. They may stay up late engaged in any number of activities only to have to get up very early for school. Lack of sleep contributes to short tempers and makes learning difficult. Set reasonable times for "lights out." If he is still up too late, you can remove the TV, phone, or computer. It's an effective and logical consequence.

Whining

Is there a cure for whining? You bet there is.

Whining is one of the ways angry children (indeed *all* children) communicate that's meant to send a message. If the whining is a signal that something is wrong, take care of that need first. If your child has resorted to whining as the only surefire way to get you to listen when you're busy, try to be more alert for the times she asks in a pleasant voice. Is she hungry? Is she bored and in need of attention? Is she lonely and could she really use some affection? Or is she tired of wandering through the store with you and needing to go home and nap? If the whining reflects a real need, ignoring it or speaking sharply in response won't help. Respond to your child's needs. Deal with the cause.

At other times, however, children whine because they've learned it gets them not what they need, but what they *want*—a toy, a treat, whatever. Each time you give in, it only hurts you and your child because it reinforces the efficacy of an annoying way to manipulate you. Rather than engage in a round of nagging/whining/nagging, help your child practice a better way of communicating and attach a consequence to the whining.

Here, role-playing can be a useful technique in teaching your child a nice way to ask for things. Make it a game. You'll need a tray with a few simple objects on it. In a playful way, demonstrate the two ways of asking for things—once with a whining tone and then in a regular, moderate tone of voice.

Have her ask for a number of the objects, again once in a whining tone, then using a "nice" voice. Teach her that when she asks with a whine, you'll give her a reminder. The second time she asks with a whine, the answer will be "No for now." Do this a few times until you're sure she understands the rule. When she asks nicely, hand over the object.

Finally, put it into practice. Remind her once that whining isn't acceptable, then reply "No for now" if she persists. If you were used to giving in or getting angry with her, it will take time for *both* of you to change old habits. But remember the four R's—request, reason, remind, and respond—discussed in Chapter 8.

Dawdling

One of the most effective weapons in the passive-aggressive child's arsenal is dawdling. Does your child pick up and inspect everything along the way? It makes you feel like saying, "Come on . . . let's pick up the pace." Young or inquisitive children need more time and parents would do well just to allow for more time.

Sometimes, dawdling is a child's way of experiencing his fascinating world. But as children grow, the dawdling could be procrastinating. They try to get one more game in at the computer or watch the rest of the TV show. At those times, a parent may need to take action. Try getting them started earlier in whatever task they need to accomplish (getting ready for bed, for example). Suggest your child tape the TV program if it's that important. Ultimately, you may need to restrict video game or TV time if these continue to be factors in tardiness.

You might do well to remind your child, "As soon as that show is over, it will be time to leave, so pack up your book bag during the commercial." Set specific time limits for the child who asks to be allowed to finish "just one more game." A fourteen-year-old I know was so good at video games that he could make a single game last another hour, so set the limits that fit your child.

Swearing

Have you lapsed into language that's perhaps been questionable during those frustrating moments with your angry child? Worse yet, has your innocent child begun to emulate your vocabulary at the most inopportune times?

People who let the wrong word fly on occasion aren't evil. But if swearing has become a problem in your house, you need to look at the root cause, and often that cause lies within a child's home. If you can honestly say you never utter anything questionable, then examine the situations in which your child is placed. She may even hear swearing at a friend's house, from peers, from grandparents, or on television.

The first part of changing a bad habit is to be aware of it. Having identified the problem, you're already on the right track, but the trouble with bad habits is that they have a way of sneaking back. Work with your child to create a plan for stamping out bad language that includes reminding one another whenever each breaks the no-swearing rule.

Second, there must be consequences for swearing. In the name of fairness, you should both take part in this, and the consequence should be immediate. Some families collect a fine each time the no-swearing rule is violated. Charge your child and yourself a dime, quarter, or dollar every time one of you says those forbidden words. Give the money to a charity so that neither one of you benefits from the fines.

Third, practice a new behavior in its place. You and your child can pretend you're facing one of those times you might be tempted to let loose with an expletive or two. Come up with another word and practice it. It might even be something silly that breaks the tension (since swearing usually occurs when something frustrates us). Break the old habit by replacing it with another action. You might even try to remind yourself to have patience.

Take a stand when the habit first appears or you'll find yourself in an embarrassing moment when your child lets loose with a few profanities at the most inopportune moment. If you nip it in the bud, you'll save lots of money in fines.

Mealtime Misery

No one wants to eat amidst tension. It certainly doesn't make for pleasant atmosphere or easy digestion. If every meal is a battleground and you seriously worry about your child's nutritional intake, it's time to use alternative strategies at the table.

Look at the messages you send about food and eating. Do you enforce an ironclad rule that absolutely every morsel must be eaten? Do you insist children eat foods that they've already expressed a hesitation toward? Maybe it's okay to refuse some selections on that night's menu, but then you aren't the kitchen of the Ritz-Carlton either. You prepare what you believe will be a balanced diet that will appeal to various family members, but be realistic. Most children don't revel in vegetables. Indeed, children's taste buds are more sensitive, so you're engaging in a pointless argument if you force a four-year-old to adore brussels sprouts. Try something sweeter instead like carrots, or puree a vegetable with potatoes or a bit of yogurt.

With younger children, creativity makes mealtime happy, not miserable. It doesn't take that much effort to cut a sandwich into an interesting shape with a cookie cutter. Sneak some veggies into a pot of chili. Kids love to dip, so take advantage of this inclination with low-fat, sweet yogurt dips that offer fun as well as calcium and good nutrition.

Try something different. Order takeout and have a picnic on the living room floor. Occasionally offer breakfast foods for dinner. When eating out, pick a family-oriented restaurant where crayons provided to children are considered to be as necessary as the utensils. Sit by a window so your child can look outside. Ask that the drink be delivered with the meal so your child doesn't fill up first on liquid. And if you must wait in an exceedingly long line to be seated, it's best to bail out.

Aside from the food, an important part of mealtime is family togetherness. Family rituals like meals and holiday traditions give kids a solid foundation. Use the time to be together. No television, no taking the meal off to their rooms. Ask the kids questions and include them in the conversation. Avoid long adult conversations that leave the child out. Use this time to focus on the importance of being a family. Catch each other up on family news. Keep it a pleasant time to be together, and you may find children actually look forward to mealtime.

Homework Hassles

Children who become underachievers are often so frustrated with school that they shut down. Anger especially plays a big role since they may have given up to defend themselves against failure, or they may take a passive-aggressive posture toward their homework.

When a child's self-esteem hits rock bottom they'd rather take the punishment for not trying than to face failure after trying. Consequently, punishment alone appears to have little effect on underachievers. It gives a frustrated child the illusion of control to say, "I could have done better if I had studied, but I didn't want to," but she may just be denying her own pain. Some kids express it a little differently by saying, "It's no use trying, I'll just flunk anyway, so why put in the work?" Whatever the reason, punishment alone will not help them turn the corner and see improvement.

Some underachievers will take out their frustrations on other children. They may resent classmates who get good grades and even bully them, as if to say, "You may get A's but I got *you*!" Again, when problems have reached this level, you may need to seek help from the school principal or a counselor. Parents should be very careful how they act toward successful students and adults, as it serves as a model for their children. The parent who frequently criticizes successful people is teaching not only an unkind message, but also a dangerous one.

Parents also battle with overachievers. These children are so driven to perform better and achieve more that grades get linked with their self-worth and they cease to enjoy schoolwork. The self-applied pressure to perform keeps their tempers near the flashpoint. Spotting stress in overachievers can help parents. Watch out for anger associated with studying, restless sleep from worrying about grades, and overreacting to even the slightest mistakes. These children need help with their view about themselves, coupled with a reality check. If your child received a low grade because she didn't study, then she must study better the next time. But if she tried her best and wasn't perfect, it's important for you to be supportive of her efforts, nonetheless.

Sloppy study habits are another cause of school problems and homework hassles. These children want to do well but simply don't know how. Criticism and nagging make things worse and lead to angry battles. Careless students need practical tips on how to study, not punishment or constant criticism. If you're not able to spend the time, or if it ends up in an argument, find him a regular tutor. Better study habits, organizational skills, and building learning skills are all lessons a tutor can teach.

Better organization is crucial to getting homework and assignments done in a timely fashion. When your child gets home, make sure he has his assignment sheet, books, and necessary papers. You may need to do daily inspections until he gets in the habit of being prepared. If he's missing something, promptly take him back to school or contact a classmate to get what he needs. Working parents who aren't home after school will need to devise a phone chain of classmates for this contingency.

Set a time for your child to start homework. You can allow for an after-school break, but then it's time to work. Kids do need to shoot hoops and burn off restless energy, or grab a snack, but don't allow them to plop down mindlessly in front of the television. If your children have become accustomed to blowing off homework, you'll have to be firm to build better study habits. Make it clear that learning time comes before playtime, which means that TV, toys, and outdoor play are all on hold until the work gets done. Check the homework and make sure it's in the folder, ready to take to school the next day, before giving the all-clear. And don't forget to praise kids for a job well done.

You *can* successfully turn a child around from "I forgot my homework" or "Everybody else flunked the test" to "Look, Mom, I aced this assignment!" If your child gets caught in one of those negative, self-fulfilling prophecies we learned of earlier in the book, remind him of the "greats" in our society. It's said that Walt Disney was fired once by a newspaper editor for his lack of ideas. But he persisted. It's said of Isaac Newton that he did poorly in school, and that Albert Einstein's teachers questioned if he would amount to anything. They persisted. Abraham Lincoln had little to no schooling. He persisted. Teach your children the pattern here, and perhaps they'll be inspired to work hard and resist the temptation to give up.

These anecdotes as well as your own could have profound impact and turn your child's negative attitude into a positive one. My co-author told me of a discussion she had with one of her sons who was down about his report card and doubted his ability to succeed. Loriann told him that as a young girl, she too got several low marks in reading, English, and social studies. Well, these days you can't keep Loriann from books, and indeed she writes them, including one on American history! In my own studies, would you believe I got a D on my first college psychology test? Well, it sure woke me up. Sometimes when we dare to share our own circuitous path to success, our children aren't afraid to overcome their own learning difficulties.

Raising a Reader

Why discuss reading in a book about angry children? First, reading can greatly influence your child's success in life. Reading is also a subject that requires attention and quiet time, and sometimes angry or impulsive children struggle with this subject far and above any others assigned in school. Additionally, reading promotes comfort and relaxation, as opposed to the potentially aggressive behaviors we discussed in the chapter on media.

Surround kids with books and reading material. Encourage them to read magazine and newspaper articles on topics that interest them, and teach them how to look up information. If your child always puts off reading, or gets angry each time you ask him to pick up a book, gather material electronically (a shared activity providing one-on-one time that's so crucial), print it out, and ask him to read it back to you at a later time.

Build in regular trips to the library or bookstore from an early age, ideally from infancy forward. Children who have been consistently exposed to books develop bigger vocabularies, have a more positive attitude toward reading, and perform better in school.

Make reading part of the family routine. Set aside a quiet time each day, maybe before bed. In fact, earlier in this chapter there are sections about bedtime battles, and reading to children can help to calm them and foster a sense of closeness between parent and child. Tie in rewards to reading if you want, although reading on its own should be reward enough. Since many an argument has surfaced over the perceived injustice of limiting video games, reading could be an incentive for more game time. The more books read, the more time one can earn. Remember, in the bigger picture of your child's life and coping skills, books can provide comfort and a path to solutions when problems arise. Reading is a far better alternative for the angry child—or truly for any child—than many alternatives that compete for their time.

Outings and Travel

Who hasn't suffered the embarrassment of having their child lose control in some public place, such as the grocery store? While all children may suffer a meltdown occasionally, for the angry child it is more than a once-in-a-while occurrence. Learning to watch for the warning signs as discussed earlier in the book can reduce the frequency of such outbursts, but if time or other pressures prevent you from acting, here are some strategies for coping:

Limit the opportunities for meltdowns. It may be inconvenient, but if a stress-free errand is your priority, best to fit it in when your child is in school, or with another parent or caregiver. It's not always apparent, however, when a storm is brewing inside your child; there are times when your child will be an angel in the car and a devil once inside some establishment's automatic doors. And it's not always possible to avoid such outings entirely. You need to be prepared.

With young children, distraction works well, as you converse and get the child involved in the shopping activity. Even while she's strapped into the cart seat at the grocery store, you might hold up two flavors or brands to elicit a smile or nod. If the choices are of little consequence, go with your child's choice. She'll feel excited that you asked her opinion and validated when you put the item in the cart. You can also ask leading questions to distract your junior shopper, such as, "Don't you think it would be fun to make popcorn tonight?" Meanwhile, you know your ulterior motive is to buy the healthier package rather than the butter-laden variety. That's okay, because you're making your shopping trip (not to mention your child's snacks) as fun and interesting as you possibly can.

Older children can appreciate the consumer economics lesson in shopping trips, particularly if you state the facts in a watertight but polite way. "This cereal might seem appealing because of its package, but if we purchase it at $4.25 a box instead of this store brand, then we can't also buy . . ." Teach them to read the shelf stickers to help identify the best buys, and show them what criteria you use in making your decisions. If they're involved, they'll have less time to become edgy and whiny.

Whenever possible, use the candy-free aisles in the grocery store, and register your children in the in-store playrooms or child-care centers if these are available to you.

For other outings where long periods of waiting may be involved, bring along your own toys, books, or snacks from home. Kids will keep busy and not notice as many of the enticements that cost you money (and sanity). Define ahead of time what constitutes good behavior. If kids balk at sitting in a car seat or using a seat belt, refuse to move the car until there's compliance on everyone's part. Calmly explain the safety rules and laws that you as parent must be responsible for obeying, and as the driver, tell them it's your job. Reward good behavior with a sincere thank-you, as in, "Thanks for behaving so well. It made it easier for me to drive through this traffic, and you helped me very much."

Especially on long car trips, create a car kit that includes books, toys, music, and headphones/portable tape players. On long road trips, listen to some of the kid's music throughout the car's stereo system instead of always swaying to your favorite tunes. And keep your expectations realistic for all travel opportunities. It's not wise to book a flight at dawn when you've got youngsters to get ready. But if that's your only option, get them to bed early and pack the car before you wake them up. Similarly, if you fail to pack a change of clothes or to remember the stroller, you can't be too disappointed in your child if they have an accident or get tired of walking long distances.

Curfews and Cars

Because of the very real possibility of injury, and because of all the desirable intangibles (freedom, maturity, mobility) driving a car represents, teens and parents will inevitably clash over use of the family car. Help her to understand that driving the car is a privilege, not a constitutional right. Establish from the outset the importance of responsible behavior. Point out that teens indeed have a higher incidence of automobile accidents. (In fact, it's the leading cause of death for teenagers.) Driving is not to be taken lightly.

Be a part of driver training. Parents who supervise forty to fifty hours of driving time greatly reduce their children's accident rate. If your child shows anger on the road, you'll need to increase your surveillance of her driving and/or reduce the privilege. And don't forget to watch your own behavior behind the wheel. If you're prone to losing your cool on the road, your child may follow right in your tracks. An additional means of teaching auto responsibility is to insist that your child have a financial stake in it, even if you can afford to pay all the expenses associated with her driving. Ask for contributions toward the cost of the vehicle, gas, insurance, and maintenance.

Many states have rules about how late kids can be on the road at night. Know these rules, and stick with them. If kids violate curfew, follow through on cutting back their auto privileges. And if you're presented with the argument, "But Jamie's parents let her stay out later," remember to keep your calm and focus. You are responsible for your *own* children. Acknowledge that you'll consider that point of view, but that you also have your own thoughts on the matter, motivated by safety concerns. You can decide if there is a grace period for being late, especially if there is a good reason, and/or if he made an attempt to get in touch with you. But avoid making this the standard practice or else you'll be creating a pattern of rewarding him for making excuses.

Friends and Trust

What teenager hasn't wanted to push the rules a little and overstay his curfew at a party or nighttime outing? When your child was younger, you probably welcomed the occasional reprieve of a sleepover at a friend's house; now that he's older, you wonder what's going on at these parties that makes them so irresistible.

The tremendous influence peer groups have on our children isn't to be taken lightly. As they mature, children discover what it means to be popular or, sadly, the opposite. They'll develop bonds with their friends that seem to supplant those with you and other relatives.

That's okay. But children still need to know there are limits. If there's ever any doubt as to what your son and his buddies are doing when the other kid's parents aren't home, you have every right to express your hesitation. Make it clear that you need to know more about the family or the situation (party invitation, sleepover, etc.) before granting your approval. You might even try having your son or daughter earn your trust in situations where you are uneasy but it appears other kids have more latitude, perhaps by requiring a phone call at an appointed time or by arranging to drop by and see what they're up to.

Of course, you'll most likely face some protests, maybe downright arguments, but remind them that building trust brings its own rewards, and the more you know about their activities, the more comfortable you'll be.

When Relatives Interfere

Well-intentioned relatives and family friends not only meddle in our matters, but thwart our best-laid plans to discipline children effectively. This can go either way. They may remember what it was like with stricter parents who spanked and never heard of having a time-out. On the other hand, they may side with your child, pitting her against her parents. If you don't deal with the occasional interference of relatives, however well intended, you may very well be driving home from Grandma's with an ornery child. When it leads to inconsistency in enforcing rules, rewarding tantrums, and being manipulated by anger, then you have a problem.

Every parent gets advice from their own family or the in-laws. When an extended family member takes over without a parent's approval, that parent worries that his or her authority will be lessened in the child's mind. The next time parent and child confront the same issue, the parent's rules are weakened, expectations get muddled, and confusion reigns. The parent's power to discipline is diminished.

Decide how any unsolicited advice fits with how you're trying to raise your child. If you've got a child who constantly manipulates you to get out of chores, then Grandma's advice to "go ahead and advance him his allowance" may not fit. Take the time to talk things over with these relatives. You may both learn from each other, and you might develop an ally in the process.

Realize also, when there are meddling relatives, that you might still be seeking the approval of your own parents. This too can interfere with efforts to discipline. Did you never quite receive the recognition you needed from your own mom or dad? Are you avoiding their advice because you still have your own personal issues with them that prevent you from being able to listen objectively? If you grew up with constant criticism, you might still be locked into attempts to resolve that issue. But don't make the mistake of putting your need for approval above your child's needs to learn anger management, abide by limits, and, above all, respect your role as parent.

Chapter Ten

Divorce Wars

W E'VE ALL heard the statistics. Fifty percent of first marriages and sixty percent of
remarriages end in divorce. According to a Census
Bureau report from 1998, approximately 10 percent
of adults (19.4 million) have been divorced. The
consequence of all these dissolved marriages is that
28 percent (twenty million) of all children under age
eighteen lived with a single parent, usually their
mother.

These statistics quantify what most of us already
know: Millions of children live in the wake of bitter-
ness between their parents, and in my practice, I see
that manifest as guilt, sadness, and especially anger.

Many parents maintain that after divorce their
lives are richer, fuller, more peaceful and positive,
because their problem marriages ended. This may
very well be the case, especially where there has been
abuse, desertion, or a real breakdown in communication. However, when children are part of the equation, divorce is rarely if ever an unalloyed blessing.

Make no mistake about it—divorce has a profound influence on the children involved. If your world was turned upside down, wouldn't you react with at least a small measure of anger?

Research has proven that divorce impacts negatively upon every area of children's development, affecting their social, emotional, and learning skills. Some parents find ways to soften the pain and successfully help their children bypass problems. Overall, however, children of divorce experience higher rates of depression, inappropriate sexual conduct, drug abuse, behavior problems, school difficulties, and delinquency.

Mere mention of the word "divorce" conjures up the most distressing images families will ever know. It's not just the end of a troubled marriage, but for many the beginning of a long and treacherous road to recovery. It's especially difficult for the children, who are powerless to bring parents back together, end the arguments, and stabilize their lives. At least in the short term, most children face some level of psychological difficulties. How parents handle divorce makes a world of difference.

Resolving Parental Issues

Fortunately, the long-term outcome of divorce does not have to be dismal. Many families can recover from divorce and may actually draw strength from their experiences. Parents have the power to make this so.

"If you had told me fifteen years ago that I would ever have recovered from my parents' divorce, I would have called you a liar," said Don, a twenty-five-year-old businessman. "But over the years, I watched how they were committed to helping us kids do well. There was a lot of pain and suffering along the way, but they made it work." If you have ended your marriage or are in the process of doing so, be especially alert to the warning signs of anger in your child and make a concerted effort to shield her from the inevitable conflicts that will arise over finances, visitation, and other practical matters. Don't force your child to choose sides or support you in your grievances against your ex-spouse. Never forget that your union can be unraveled, but your child's bond to her parents cannot, and the damage done to that relationship will harm your child as intensely as it harms your ex-spouse.

Now more than ever, it's your job to put your child's priorities first. Unless communications have broken down entirely, try to work with your spouse to resolve and redefine the myriad details of family life in such a way that your children don't bear the brunt of *your* anger and sadness. In some cases the intervention of a professional—whether a counselor or another kind of facilitator—may be useful.

Whether you go it alone or with help, the most successful transitions encompass these four elements:

- Redefining the marital relationship from copartners to coparents: As parents go through all the emotional turmoil of divorce, it's essential that you recommit yourselves to your role as parents. Even if you cannot live together as a couple, you both need to make a commitment to being coparents.
- Reorganizing the household (work, housing, finances) and establishing stability: It's a strain to take on more work. But it's a fact that the cooking, shopping, repairs, lawn mowing, and handling the checkbook is no longer going to be shared. Adults need to think through how they'll manage all of these new responsibilities and still have time for the kids.
- Maintaining parenting skills as children cope with the divorce and adjust to the natural developmental childhood stages: Divorcing adults are often caught up in a storm of emotions, but so are the kids. Parents must recognize the importance of being there for the kids' needs regardless of their own turmoil. Whether it's reading a story, teaching her to ride a bike, or providing a shoulder to cry on, parents must be available in order to raise healthy kids. There's no doubt that it's tougher to be supportive when you're

going through so much yourself; that's why you have to make a conscious effort to be there for your children. Ask friends to remind you of this. Read books about helping your kids during this time, as well as articles about normal child development issues.

■ Making necessary adjustments to careers, social life, and health: The fourth adjustment deals with taking care of yourself. The definition of who you are at work and with friends will undergo changes. You may no longer associate with the same friends. Work and financial opportunities may change as you have to deal with issues such as child support and child visitation schedules. It's a struggle as you grow older either alone or with new partners. All of these four tasks take a lot of work, but by knowing what you'll face, you're better prepared to grow and help your child through this time.

Attention to each of these areas may ease what will inevitably be a painful transition. Remember too that if you truly feel blocked, continually sad or angry, professional counseling might help you to move on. Whatever help you receive to heal your pain will benefit your child as well.

Dealing with Your Own Anger

Frequently, the divorcing adults are blind to the anger that underlies their personal situation. I've worked with many ex-couples who deny their anger, although their bitter emotions are clearly visible to those around them. Conflicts between parents hurt the children in several ways. For starters, the child may be acting out emotions that the whole family feels but can't bring themselves to articulate. In this case, it's easier to come together around the child than to get help for yourself. Parents' conflicts can get in the way of consistent discipline when one parent tries to undermine the other's stance or refuses to support the other's efforts. Children often imitate the angry and aggressive actions of their parents, and can develop problems in order to distract parents away from the marital discord.

Anger also manifests itself as undermining. For example, one parent may refuse to use the title "Mom" or "Dad," opting to use first names instead. Or perhaps your daughter complains about her dad, and her mom immediately sides with her, even if she'd ordinarily agree with her ex-husband's perspective.

Another way divorced parents mismanage their anger is by ignoring visitation. If you have regular, scheduled visitation, by all means keep it as proof to the child that even though the marriage didn't last, your parental love goes on forever. My coauthor, Loriann, also wrote *Surviving Separation & Divorce.* In her book, she writes, "Children wait anxiously for the noncustodial parent to arrive. Understandably, work may prevent you from being on time, traffic may snarl your best efforts, and you do deserve to have a life outside of the parent/child relationship. But your commitment to your children is paramount. . . . Unfortunately, this is an area marred by late-show or no-show parents, often in an effort to infuriate their estranged partner or prove a point." Whether undermining exists through open warfare, verbal slights, or passive-aggressive actions, it's detrimental to your child. If you're divorced or in the process, self-analyze your behavior as best you can, correcting it if you spot any signs.

Children Caught in the Cross Fire

Judith S. Wallerstein is considered a leading authority on the effects of divorce. She founded the Center for the Family in Transition in California, and wrote about her studies in several books, including her most recent twenty-five-year study on the effects of divorce upon children.[13] In her earlier book, *Second Chances,* Wallerstein has described seven tasks kids face in coping with divorce:[14]

- Understanding what divorce means in the family
- Getting back to their own activities
- Coming to terms with the loss of their parents' marriage
- Taking care of their own anger
- Handling guilt or feelings that they caused the marriage's demise
- Accepting the permanence of divorce
- Learning to take risks for future success and loving relationships

Parents are the best resource to help their child work through these tasks. As we all understand, marriage takes effort. Divorce requires as much or more.

There are factors that can help us predict which children will have greater adjustment concerns. Those from homes with high levels of conflict after the divorce face a tougher time since it's hard to adjust when parents themselves are angry and argumentative. Whatever psychological symptoms children experienced before the separation are good predictors of the kinds of symptoms they'll have later on. And of course, a child's age and emotional development are fundamental.

The Range of Children's Reactions

Whether parents divorce calmly or bitterly, children may show a wide range of emotional reactions. Some children are relieved that the arguments may end with the parents' separation, but most children don't react this way. They may act more frustrated, impatient, or anger easily. Children may become depressed, withdrawn, or moody. To cope with the stresses, a child may even deny their parents are splitting up.

Even when they've been the victims of abuse, children may show grief over the divorce. The loss of a bad parent is still the loss of *a* parent. A child may have lived for a long time with the wish that things could have been worked out another way, and thus will mourn the loss of the fantasy parent.

Schoolwork suffers for some children, while others may show an improvement in their grades. There may be less time to study, since the child is shuttled back and forth between houses. Parents may not have consistent study demands. Some children purposely do poorly as an expression of anger. Other children's grades improve as a result of the reduced tension, or they may study more to escape from the pressures, or in an attempt to be the ideal child.

Behavior changes often accompany separation and divorce. A young child's tantrums and crying can increase. Disobedience may occur in another child as an expression of anger and resentment. Rude and disrespectful talk may emerge in a child who had been charming before the divorce. The mother of two teenagers told me that her teens seemed to constantly order her about and criticize her. When she asked why they talked that way, her daughter said, "Dad told us you talked that way to him, so you deserve it." Dad taught the kids to blame Mom for the divorce and take out their anger on her.

Occasionally, children try to be extra perfect, and extremely helpful around the house. This pattern occurs when children hope to rescue their parents' marriage. They may feel if they clean the house and are good kids, their parents wouldn't have anything left to fight about. This thinking turns a child into an angel on the outside, but inside he is constantly frustrated that his method isn't working. And as you can guess, that frustration leads to anger.

Age Influences Reactions

A child's emotional reactions to divorce are tied to his age. Infants can react with a sense of helplessness, while preschoolers may blame themselves. Expect some regression in terms of accomplished milestones (such as toilet-training problems or separation anxiety).

School-age children might respond with anger and sadness. They may have fears about being left, fears about a parent's safety (especially if there is domestic violence involved), and conflicts over loyalty to one parent or another. Adolescents can develop an air of false maturity or sink into themselves, almost becoming recluses. It helps to keep these reactions in mind when dealing with the fallout from a divorce.

Children of different ages express their frustration very differently. Tears or fears expressed by a child with divorcing parents don't necessarily mean that one parent is harming or abusing the child. But as we'll read further in this chapter, a parent's actions can contribute directly to the child's response.

Older children may feel a very real pressure to grow well beyond their years. They may take on adult tasks around the house or may try to be your best friend to make you feel better. Adolescents and teenagers might understand all too well the financial pinch you could be suffering, and fear the viability of their own college plans, especially given that parental obligations often cease when children turn eighteen. Watching a college-educated parent turn his back on providing a similar future for his children makes children bristle and become angry.

This age group may become very uncomfortable with your new-found sexuality when it comes to establishing yourself in the dating arena. And as Judith Wallerstein points out, many adult children of divorce are ill-equipped at choosing romantic partners suitable to their own needs. They might fall into the first relationship that avails itself, and without a model of how to negotiate conflict appropriately within a marriage, their own unions suffer when trouble strikes (as it inevitably will). The first tendency might be to bail out, leaving these children all the more distraught facing another loss.

Finally, if there is any revelation regarding one parent's character, older or adult children will most likely take notice. Kids want their parents to be the good guys. Therefore, they'll feel unsettled to learn of misdeeds or unpleasant circumstances no matter what age.

Games Parents Play

I was talking with a group of children who came from recently divorced families. They were complaining about the games parents play to split them against the other parent—games that lead to hurt and anger. Honestly, after hearing these heartfelt concerns, it struck me. At perhaps no other time in my years as a psychologist have I wanted to take a parent aside, look them square in the eye and say, "Will you *please* grow up." That's because parents are often blinded to what they're doing during divorce. I'll share the thoughts of these children, as I couldn't have said it any better myself:

- Please don't criticize or complain about Mom (or Dad). And when you're unhappy with us, please don't tell us we're just like our father/mother. That hurts because we know you didn't like them. Does that mean you'll want to get rid of us too?
- No matter how mad you feel about the divorce, it doesn't mean Mom (or Dad) is all bad. Please say something good about them once in a while so we don't feel we have to keep our feelings a secret.
- When we tell you we had fun at Dad's (or Mom's) house, please don't ignore it or make a face like it's not possible. We don't want to lie to you and tell you it was awful just so you feel better.
- We're not spies. Please don't give us the grand inquisition each time we arrive at your house after a visit with them.
- If you feel we are wrongly complaining too much about Mom (or Dad), then correct us. We want you to act like a parent and tell us if we're doing something wrong.
- Don't start fights with Mom (or Dad) when we kids are around. Save it until we're not there.
- Don't send messages through us to them. If you aren't grown-up enough to say it yourself, how do you expect kids to do it right?
- We're kids. Just as we're not messengers, we're not your best friend, your therapist, your lawyer, or even the judge.

- Please stop trying to buy our love with lots of presents. We'd rather spend happy times with you.
- Don't prevent us from contact with Mom (or Dad). You may not like her, but we still might, despite the situation. Similarly, don't abandon us just because it's hard to pick us up at the house or run into Mom. Just deal with it. Like we have to.
- And please stop asking us which parent we want to live with. What we really want is for parents to get along. If you adults can't solve your problems, how are we kids supposed to do it?

Common Divorce Problems

I'll elaborate on a few of the concerns these children outlined, and since many divorced parents do move on to future relationships, I'll tackle that issue as well.

CURBING CONFLICT

There are many ways parents place their child in the middle of adult battles. They might use the child as a messenger, for instance. While it may seem harmless to say, "Tell your dad that you must be home at five instead of seven on Sunday," that simple message can lead to several problems. For example, what if the child forgets to tell Dad—who is to blame? What if Dad had plans that lasted past five o'clock? Who gets to decide what happens with the schedule? Where is the child going that's more important than spending time with Dad?

Without direct communication between parents, too much can be misinterpreted. The child messenger often hears the negative response first. The other parent may mistakenly respond, out loud, "Oh yeah, who does she think she is to tell me what to do?" or something similar.

To spare the child from being put in this position, parents should speak directly. If that's impossible, use an intermediary, someone you've both agreed to speak through. Or in this age of electronic mail, sending brief details back and forth eliminates personal conversation that might degenerate into an attitude. Other problems exist when communication is overtly one-sided. That is, you never get any feedback to e-mail or answers to direct questions. Again, this withholding from one parent to another is often passive-aggressive anger. You can only control your own behavior, so make sure this isn't your communication style.

Another way of involving your child in the conflict is to criticize the other parent with the intent of turning your child against him or her. You can answer your child's questions about the divorce in terms he can understand at his age, but be very careful about the information you share. Explaining that you and your former spouse had problems is one thing. Telling your child that his other parent was bad is quite another. If your relationship was abusive, you may feel the need to help your child see the differences between healthy and unhealthy relationships, but keep in mind you are walking a fine line. If your motive is to hurt your child's relationship with the other parent, it is best to keep quiet. In most cases, harmful information about the other parent does not need to be shared with the child. If you are unsure how to handle it, talk it over first with someone who can give you an objective opinion.

CUSTODY AND VISITATION WOES

Stresses that stem from visitation include a child's adjustments to a new house, neighborhood, and friends. Parents orient their child to a new environment by walking them through it and getting the child involved in local activities. This helps to make the new area a part of the child's life. Many separated parents try to maintain homes close to each other in order to reduce the disruption in their kids' lives. It also makes it easier for the kids to hop on a bike for impromptu visits.

Conversely, some parents purposefully move farther away to make it difficult for the other parent to visit. Life may indeed force parents and stepfamilies to make changes, but moving just to hurt the other parent can hurt the child as well. In another difficult situation, I've seen other families separate, at least initially, under one roof. This can prove confusing to children, who see the arrangement as not that different from their intact family. In cases of ongoing discord, abuse, or other problem behaviors, I wouldn't advise that parents try to separate and live in the same residence.

Sure, visitation can be stressful when the two households have different rules. If one house abhors a mess while the other permits it, your child will inevitably comment, "But Dad doesn't mind if I eat in front of the TV," which leads to arguments between the other parent and child. Avoid the comparisons and help your child accept that different homes have different rules.

OTHER CONSEQUENCES

Child-rearing techniques are balanced when there are two parents. Divorced mothers and fathers often have to do that balancing themselves, as single parents. Thinking also gets clouded when one parent doesn't trust the other. To alleviate some of the decision-making burden, at least consult with another adult whom you do trust. Think about the best rules for your child. Think about how you might be overreacting or not looking at the broader picture. Very often, an impartial friend (preferably one with knowledge of children) can validate you and take a great burden from your shoulders.

Finally, discipline suffers if parents relax the rules for fear the children will reject them. But children still need consistent limits. The rules provide stability and consistency for a child whose world has taken a tumble.

Starting New Relationships

When dating enters the picture for a divorced mom or dad, children must adapt. Unfortunately, some children will become withdrawn or openly angry. While some children latch on to their parent's new significant other with great excitement at being a family again, other kids resent their parent's dating. These children might see this new boyfriend or girlfriend as standing in the way of the parents' reconciliation. Older children might fear the rampant stereotypes they've surely heard, such as the younger woman out for their father's investments, or they might be afraid they'll be forgotten in the midst of step-siblings (or worse yet, new children born into the union).

Children sense a parent's anger and jealousy toward their former spouse's paramour. They may feel that if they like this person, they're betraying the other parent. So they learn to keep their feelings a secret or to side with one parent against the other. Either situation stresses the child. If possible, each parent should give their son or daughter permission to like the other parent's boyfriend/girlfriend, husband/wife. This relieves distress and keeps lines of communication open.

But use some common sense. Don't flaunt new relationships. First, your kids will sense an air of showing off, particularly if it's aimed at antagonizing their other parent. Second, it risks the child's attachment process. If she gets too attached to someone you eventually break up with, it's an unpleasant replay of your divorce all over again, at least from the child's perspective. Third and finally, flaunting is not good modeling.

I've heard from kids themselves who know darn well what it means to be plopped in front of the television while Dad and his new girlfriend moan behind closed doors. The sounds that emanate force children to deal with sexual subjects they might not have had to deal with as soon. Quite frankly, these parents need to get themselves under control. Children of divorce are often startled to see their parents as sexual persons. From a teenager's perspective, it may seem downright weird to watch Dad primp for a date or Mom be kissed good night at the same time they're exploring their own teen experiences with dating. The entire subject elicits sexual fantasies in some children, and causes embarrassment in others.

This isn't to say that divorced parents shouldn't move into new relationships. They should. Merely keep them private until they look like they will last. Sometimes the motives behind quick introductions are meant to create jealousy or a "watch me" attitude to the exspouse. Introduce a new girlfriend or boyfriend gradually. In other words, a sudden onslaught of activities or meals with this new person can be a little daunting. Stretch these meetings out, and don't make too much of them.

Realize also that as these partners become permanent, forming a stepfamily can be difficult for children, particularly if their needs take a backseat to the budding romance or a new family. Reassure children in blended families that they will always be important, and that you strive toward fairness and wish to keep communication open. Often, this is enough to prevent angry outbursts or behavioral problems.

Advice Parents Must Try

For separated or divorced parents, this list may provoke thought, discussion, and hopefully help you understand how divorce impacts a child's anger:

- Don't be too quick. If you're uncertain about separation, read some of the books recommended in the appendix. Even if dissolving your marriage is the best outcome, you'll be more prepared. Don't hesitate to discuss your feelings with a counselor.
- Do break the news as gently as possible. In Vicky Lansky's *Divorce Book for Parents,* she likens the mention of divorce to shouting "Fire" in a crowded room. Parents are a packaged deal, she points out. Kids never anticipate having two homes, two sets of clothes, two bikes, or perhaps even four sets of grandparents. While being as honest as possible about the pain, choose your words carefully (reviewing the tips on parental anger earlier in this chapter).
- Do give necessary assurances. Reassure your child often that the breakup is not his or her fault. Do this regardless of your child's

age. If you've got young children, you can get a copy of the Mister Rogers booklet "Talking with Families About Divorce" (see Recommended Resources for the mailing address).

■ Do watch what you say. Refrain from judgmental labels like "bimbo," "jerk," or "deadbeat," and don't get too technical with legal jargon. Words like "custody" and "child support" aren't even in your child's lexicon. But do be honest, especially if there will be some changes in lifestyle, a move to another residence or school, or other very obvious consequences. Never lie, bribe, or promise (remember, the indulging family contributes to a child's anger).

■ Do consider therapy or education. Do this for both yourself and your children. Gary Neuman's Sandcastles program is court-ordered in many jurisdictions. This innovative approach, outlined in *Helping Your Kids Cope with Divorce the Sandcastles Way,* guides children through the maze of marital trauma. Parents attend their own educational sessions to learn ways of mediating disputes, as well as the effect divorce will have on their children, including childhood depression.

■ Do try formal mediation. This is usually a lot more cost-effective for parents than litigating custody and visitation issues, and less adversarial. A mediator listens to both sides to work out cooperative agreements on issues of finances, visitation, and parenting skills. (However, mediation is not generally effective in cases of domestic violence, where there is an unequal balance of power as well as control issues.)

■ Do reconcile with extreme vigilance. Your children may hold on to false hopes that the two of you will reconcile. The worst case is that their hopes will be dashed twice, and you'll have to pick up their pieces all over again. The best case is that they'll have an intact family once more, but until you feel there is real hope, perhaps you and your estranged should meet for dates without the children knowing about it.

■ Do know your children's friends. All kids, even adolescents, need to feel a part of a crowd. If they see their family unraveling, their crowd could very well be a clique you don't approve of. At older ages, it's not uncommon to see experimentation with drugs, alcohol, or sexual relations.

■ Do protect childhood. Indeed, there will be more to do around the house, and times of loneliness. While there's nothing wrong with kids pitching in, you don't want to burden them with adult chores. Avoid making your children your confidantes. This forces them to grow beyond their years and capabilities.

■ Do remain consistent, especially with discipline, household routines, and shows of affection. Kids of all ages need consistency. They want and need you to be the parent, modeling appropriate anger management yourself. It may surprise you, but they also want limits for their own misbehavior. Feel free to reiterate the resounding message of this book—it's sometimes okay to be angry, but never okay to be mean. (And try to keep daily routine interruptions to a minimum.)

■ Do support their relationship with the other parent. Even if the other parent has some traits you don't like, don't interfere with your child's bonds.

■ Do stay connected to your kids. Realize that boys require your being there, and girls like to talk more. Your son might open up if you agree to shoot a few hoops. Both sons and daughters will appreciate your attendance at school functions, so keep a calendar and make these a priority.

■ Don't withhold extras. Every child deserves a few extras in this world. By extras, I mean the chance to go to summer camp, be in scouts or the band, take swim lessons, and receive tutoring if necessary. Add in preschool and a college education if your children are older. Some angry parents withhold extras from their children when they're clearly able to provide them, either financially or in terms of making schedule adjustments to shuttle them off to practice, lessons, etc. Don't assume the custodial parent can provide all of these perks to your child out of the child support you may pay. If it's within your reach to help provide these, do it. These are your children, and a few extras bring nothing but benefit to them.

Many children are hurt by divorce, but many also survive. Parents often decide how that will turn out. While Mom and Dad cannot escape the pain of divorce, they can be sensitive to children's feelings, putting the kids first.

Chapter Eleven

The Road to Positive Parenting

A PATIENT NAMED Martha arrived frazzled, weary, and thirty minutes late for her appointment. She needed to talk for it had been a bad day. A very bad day, as I learned. Sitting in my office that evening was her first chance to rest since six A.M.

As Martha got ready to pick up her son from school that day and take him to basketball practice, her already hectic departure was interrupted by the distinct sound of rushing water in the bathroom. Danielle, her two-year-old, had always been over-zealous when it came to toilet paper. You guessed it—the waters were flowing from a clogged commode. As Martha struggled with the plunger, their sickly dog threw up on her shoe. Four-year-old Dominic was inspired to answer nature's call but decided the bathroom was too busy a place. So he relieved himself on the hall floor. Martha hurriedly mopped the floors and changed her shoes. The clog would have to wait as she tossed coats on the children and herded them out the door.

Over the din of the dog and Dominic, she hadn't heard the phone. Who would have guessed that twelve-year-old Marty would choose this day to become conscientious? A thousand times she'd told him to call if there was a change in plans, and 999 times he forgot, until today, leaving a message that ball practice had been cancelled. To save Mom a trip, he headed home on the bus, only to have Martha waiting in the school parking lot. Hungry at home, Marty charred pizza in the oven, opening the back door to let the smoke out, and accidentally the dog as well. At the exact moment Martha arrived home, Marty headed for the bathroom and flushed the already problematic toilet! "Where does a parent even start to take care of a day like that?" Martha asked me as we began our session.

As I told Martha that evening, it is sometimes hard to remain positive about parenting without giving in to frustration and anger. How do we manage to endure the messes, the forgetfulness, the challenges that surprise us each day? Ward and June, Ozzie and Harriet, Mike and Carol Brady, heck, even Gomez and Morticia, seemed to manage life's hectic moments better than most of us. Why, they barely raised an eyebrow! But times have changed. In this new century, we need to explain to our children how people become homeless, why they die of AIDS, or why our heroes pursue self-destructive paths. I know there's yet another change in society when I'm called to comment on seemingly inexplicable teenage violence or presidential escapades. Kids are growing up in a troubled world that can make them cynical and lacking trust. With the Internet an ever-larger influence on kids, we can no longer shield them from everything, because the neighborhood is not just the block—it's the world.

The challenges of parenting change more rapidly than Madonna's hairstyle. No wonder we're so overcome by doubt. Do we spank, yell, ground, give a time-out, reward, bribe, threaten, praise, or what? And even if we do, how do we know we haven't inflicted some irreparable harm on our child?

But folks, we've got to remain positive. Upbeat. Enthusiastic. We've got to keep the faith that what we're doing is valuable and worth all our energy.

The techniques listed in this book will help, though they aren't enough to see us parents through difficult times, particularly those times when we're parenting an irritable child. But there is one more key to helping you with your angry child—the beliefs and values you live by. These will vastly influence what we fret over and what we let slide by. Knowing the difference—knowing what we care about—gives us a sense of purpose and direction in an otherwise aimless world.

Beliefs make us optimists or pessimists. They bring us hope or misery, and they either help or hinder our parenting skill. They determine if we interpret a situation with hope or helplessness. Your beliefs will help you adjust to difficult times and prevent anger from getting out of hand at home, in school, and in society at large. Positive beliefs help us focus on appropriate goals to get ahead, for ourselves and for our children. This reminds me of a man in a parenting workshop I conducted. He boasted, "My kids toe the line because they know if they ever act up they'll get smacked." He held up his right hand to show off the tool of his trade.

"But what if that doesn't work?" another parent asked.

"Oh, then I have a backup plan," he said, holding up his left hand.

This brought a chuckle until someone else asked, "If it works so well, why are you at a parenting workshop?"

His shoulders drooped as he confessed, "Because my kids have more ideas than I have hands."

Here was a man restrained by his limited options. Parenting through intimidation was getting him nowhere, except on the fast track to my workshop.

There *are* alternatives to our old standbys, and they're more likely to improve the quality of our family life. In fact, families who have built up a large repertoire of options tend to function better. A parent that is resilient enough to try a new tack when one method no longer works because the kids have caught on, or simply outgrown it, feels less trapped.

There are times to stand firm and times to change. That's why I encourage parents to share their good ideas, and to search for new ones through books, workshops, and discussion. Consider options that solve the long-term problem, not just the struggle of the moment. If your daughter has picked up a sassy vocabulary, teach talk that's respectful. It's a more reasonable goal that carries into future dealings with others while curbing the sudden choice of words. Or if your son covets the music of a nasty group, don't just dictate, "You can't listen to that." Sit down with him and review the lyrics, telling him why you find them objectionable. Help your son find better music to enjoy.

Familiar parenting axioms come to mind. "Spare the rod, spoil the child." "Children should be seen, not heard." Each family develops its own parenting beliefs and core values. What are yours? Hopefully, your beliefs are healthy, not counterproductive. We need to ask what the belief may yield in the future to determine whether it's an appropriate belief that truly reflects the outcome we desire.

Belief	Short-term Outcome	Long-term Outcome
"I can't stand it when my child has tantrums, and I'll do anything to stop it."	Tantrum stops when parent gives in	· tantrums continue · guilt of giving in · overindulgence · lack of consistency/no clear expectations for child
"If my child doesn't like it when he doesn't get his way, it's not the end of the world."	Child gets upset	· he learns you keep self-control · he learns you won't be intimidated into doing the wrong thing · you gain confidence

A parent's philosophy is shaped by experiences, the hopes and dreams held before their children were born, and the discoveries made since. Parents do have beliefs that get them into trouble and sabotage success.

The attitudes we hold are very important to our parenting. They can make the whole difference between being effective or ineffective, staying calm or losing your cool. Our attitudes and beliefs influence how we feel and how we act. When we do not have a specific technique to handle a specific situation, our beliefs are what will carry us through. That is why developing a healthy set of parenting beliefs is so critically important to handling the angry child.

Healthy Attitude #1—Teach Independence

One of the great paradoxes of parenting is that children depend upon parents to teach them to become independent. When parents do too much for their children, those kids don't learn to do much for themselves. In other words, if they're capable of doing something for themselves, let them. This includes the angry child. It might be easier, perhaps less embarrassing, to cover up and never hold your son or daughter accountable for talking back to teachers or bullying at school, or striking out at a sibling. But in so doing, you are restricting your child to a life of limited options and choices. If you smooth over the consequences of his anger, you may figure he'll get over it, and be less angry or frustrated the next time. What parents must realize is that the anger festering inside a child often lingers inside the adult he or she grows into. That same child could become the hostile mother, battering husband, or smart-mouthed employee (or boss) who never quite learned to manage a poor temper or quick tongue.

As children strive toward independence they may stumble along the way—and their parents may be tempted to fix things yet again. Sometimes you are better off letting your teenager learn on her own that her boyfriend is not Mr. Right or that spending hard-earned money on a car that will require a lot of repairs or that staying up late talking on the phone can lead to a poor test grade. There are times you have to let life teach its lessons. Stepping in all the time creates dependency. If you want your child to grow, sometimes you have to let go.

Healthy Attitude #2—Emphasize the Process and the Product

Children do well in life when they're taught to strive for success and to push themselves to do their best. It's a sign of good self-esteem when a child believes she can overcome problems and go for the proverbial gold. This holds true for angry children as well as the child with ADHD who may have to work five times as hard to study and focus as other kids, but can still succeed in school, ace tests, and earn good grades.

However, emphasizing only the final achievement isn't going to ensure success. Parents can have a stronger impact by teaching children to enjoy and respect the process of getting there. That process can mean studying for a test, practicing an instrument, playing a sport, or working on a science project. It's not just winning the game, but learning to master a new skill and growing stronger, fleeter, more competent. It's not just getting good grades, but the feeling of pride that the child learned something also.

Healthy Attitude #3—Think Like a Child

Groucho Marx said, "This would be a better world for children if parents had to eat spinach." And Fred Rogers is known to remark that parents often forget what it's like not to be able to reach the light switch. Knowing how a child thinks gives parents valuable insights about how and when to react.

I remember taking an afternoon walk with my daughter when she was young. We'd walk a few feet and she would stop to look at a stick, pick up a stone, or sometimes seemed to stand there staring at nothing. Eventually I got frustrated with her dawdling. I'd want her to hurry along, but a few feet later she'd stop again.

At first I urged her to keep moving, but her intense interest reminded me that while we take walks, children go on explorative journeys. I thought back to my own kindergarten days recalling the sense of wonder I felt when studying the color of a leaf, drawing a picture, or learning to read. Thinking about those experiences made me realize my daughter and I were taking that walk for two entirely different reasons. Similar discoveries await all parents. When we remember what teasing felt like, it helps us teach our children how to handle friendships. Recalling the anxieties of our own adolescence gives us insight into what teenagers go through. It creates a bridge of understanding between parent and child that aids us in deciding when to talk, when to listen, and when to set limits. I once helped a mom find that proverbial lightbulb moment when she realized how being dragged through women's clothing racks for a couple of hours had to be awfully boring for two young sons. Instead of punishing them for their complaints she began to leave them with a baby-sitter when she shopped. Everyone won.

Healthy Attitude #4— Choose Your Words Carefully

So often we slip into parenting jargon—you know, the phrases that have become all too familiar throughout the generations. I'd suggest replacing the phrases with some praises. When your child wants something you disapprove of and tells you her best friend has it, you ask, "If your friend jumped off a bridge, would you?"

Kids translate this question as, "You and your friends are being foolish." If you had tried a more positive verbal alternative (and got rid of the cliché), you might have gotten your message across with much less rancor. You could agree by saying, "I know Sally's family is comfortable with that choice, but we all make decisions differently and it's not a choice we're willing to make."

Sometimes parents initiate the wrong dialogue. If a father says, "I'm sick of you and the messes you make," the translation might be heard as, "Dad thinks we're slobs . . . Dad doesn't like us living here . . . we're in his way." What the kids think their father means may be very different from what he really hopes to communicate. Humor might work wonders. Dad could say, "I hear the health department is sweeping through the neighborhood—better get ready." Or he could praise by offering, "I know you want to help out your mom since she's under a lot of stress at work, so how about cleaning up a little? It would mean a lot."

Couch criticism with concern. Instead of lamenting, "What did you do *that* for?" you could just say, "I'm concerned you might be making too big a step here. Can we talk about it?"

Limit the lectures. When you were a kid, do you remember hearing those dreaded words: "When I was your age . . ." It was an immediate turnoff. Why? Because that situation probably has no bearing on your son's or daughter's life. These kids want to know how *they* can move forward, not how you did it.

It's helpful to use your own experiences as stories to let kids know you faced similar issues, or as a healthy means of sharing family history. It's not healthy to use it as another way to put down your child.

Additionally, parents can break the ice on many taboo topics, or just engage in ordinary conversation that makes communication less tension-prone, by spending time with their child. Often the mere act of paying attention to what they're doing elicits discussion that might not otherwise occur. So drive your child to soccer practice. Shoot some hoops. Ride bikes. Play a board or computer game you both enjoy. You'll be surprised at how children open up about their fears, their tears, and all that makes them angry when they feel such a connection occur.

Healthy Attitude #5—Learn to Laugh

One day in the Pennsylvania Senate, debate continued until four in the morning with both exhaustion and tempers rising. Fellow Senator Bob Jubelirer whispered to me, "You know, Tim, in the end none of this amounts to much. The only thing that matters is family." And Jacqueline Kennedy once commented, "If you bungle raising your children, I don't think whatever else you do matters very much." She was right, and so was my friend Bob. Parenting *is* a serious job.

However, I've seen many people beat themselves up emotionally for relatively minor mistakes. I've seen still others insist on perfection so that they aren't enjoying the unique gift of their children. Life is too terribly short to take every moment so seriously. Even when we mess up, the ability to laugh is healthy. Maintaining our anger, our hurt, and our grudges will blind us. Humor helps us drop our blindfold and allows us to learn. It reminds me of a couple I once saw in marriage counseling.

My patients, Ted and Lisa, often came to sessions in the midst of an argument. Ted had a really hard time managing life's stresses and was often on the verge of a blowup. He seemed remorseful, but quickly shifted the blame to his "impossible" ten- and twelve-year-old daughters, and to his wife, labeling her the "instigator."

One week, Ted recounted an incident that had occurred during one of his daughter's recent sleepovers. Around two in the morning he was awoken by laughter and giggling. Tired and once again angry, he headed downstairs, but as he got closer he heard the sound of his own voice. His daughter was showing her friends candid home videos. Ted carefully peeked into the room and heard his daughter say, "Now watch, this is where he really loses it" as her girlfriends broke out in guffaws at the video of Ted yelling frantically at the dog. Ted felt embarrassed as he realized how he had appeared to others. To me, he said, "I never realized I looked like such a fool." But as Ted continued with the story, I helped him take the severity out of it. I pointed out what he'd told me, that one of the girls commented, "Your dad is really funny," to which his eldest daughter replied, "Yeah, he's just a bit intense, but we still like him. I just hope I'm not around when his brain explodes." The point: They unconditionally loved him.

That experience helped Ted see how he looked to others, and more important, it showed him that he should learn to enjoy his daughters rather than fight with them constantly. Despite his behavior, his kids could still tell he loved them, and they loved him in return.

Healthy Attitude #6—Parent Peacefully in an Angry World

No one has come up with a parenting technique that's flawless and easy. Maybe that's the way it should be. After all, children have to learn how to live with the challenges of an imperfect, often angry world.

In the aftermath of any tragedy involving a child, many news reports cry, "Where are the parents?" I'm sure the parents of any child who has been responsible for such frightful acts are not proud, but devastated. Faced with the repercussions of their child's actions in the media glare, they're almost always stunned and hurt, trying to sort through the clues just like the rest of us. Instead of asking how the parents failed, I'd like to see us ask, "How can we love our children more fully, and lead them with appropriate limits?"

In fact, one of the keys to parenting in this often-angry era is the realization that you can love your children and still set limits. Contrary to popular opinion, angry children can't be controlled with punishment. Setting limits first, before any angry words have been exchanged or hostile acts performed, has a far greater impact on a child's behavior.

Punishment serves as a Band-Aid. Why not prevent the wound in the first place? For instance, if we yell at our children after they've hurled a racial slur or slapped a playmate, we only put a quick fix on the incident, at that moment. If we teach our children to be tolerant of one another, to communicate what's on their minds, and solve conflicts, we impart coping mechanisms and a value system that will last them a lifetime.

A Final Word

This book is a collection of insights and ideas to give you a better grasp at understanding and helping the angry child. As I said in the introduction, I had wanted to write a book about children's anger well over ten years ago—well before some kids began startling the rest of us. But while such acts grab the headlines, we'll not learn much from them if we focus solely on the anguish, rather than the answers. We're bound to feel deep emotion, as we must. I maintain, however, that after grieving we must refocus into positive action.

It's great that we can set public policy to deal with bullying or maintain zero tolerance for violence, but reaching out to children starts not in our State Houses, but in each of our families' houses. The answers to our problems start at home. Parents have more power here than a psychologist or senator.

We can quickly look to blame any single issue, but each of us has a role. Every parent that doesn't know what their child is doing with TV, video games, the Internet, school, and friends should be looking within their own family first, before looking to other influences.

Children want and need limits. Schools and parents must set them. Yes, children test the limits—that's the nature of childhood. But it's the responsibility of parents to enforce the limits, not give up because it's too hard. As a society, we have sacrificed good sense at the altar of pop psychology and have grown to stretch the boundaries too far. Some behavior may be common in children, but we must not confuse what is common with what is acceptable.

I have learned much from different families' successes and failures. Like them, I keep learning as well. While I don't claim to have all the answers, I do maintain that the level of hope for our future as a society can be measured only by the strength of our families. That's one answer I am certain about.

Parenting is a long road, sometimes bumpy, at other times smooth, and occasionally, treacherous. Traveling that road is not a sprint, it's a marathon. We have our success and failures along the way. We experience the whole range of feelings from exhaustion to exhilaration. We face days that are thoughtful and those that are thankless. It's a long road for children as well. And along that way, when a child is angry for a moment or for many months, keep in mind the strategies outlined in this book to make life better.

Even in life's darkest moments, your love and your actions make a difference in the future health and happiness of your child and, we can only hope, in the lives of other children as well. Live your life as if you make a difference in the life of a child, and indeed you will.

Notes

1. Bushman, B. J., Baumeister, R. F., and Stack, A. D. Catharsis, aggression, and persuasive influence: Self-fulfilling or self-defeating prophecies? *Journal of Personality and Social Psychology* 76(3):367–376, 1999.
2. Fava, M., Rosenbaum, J. F. Anger attacks in patients with depression. *Journal of Clinical Psychiatry* 60:21–24, 1999.
3. Eron, L. D., et al. *Reason to Hope.* American Psychological Association, 1994.
4. Birmaher, B., et al. Childhood and adolescent depression: A review of the past ten years. Part 1. *Journal of the American Academy of Child and Adolescent Psychiatry* 35:1427–1439, 1996.
5. Shaffer, D., et al. The NIMH diagnostic interview schedule for children, version 2.3 (DISC-2.3): Description, acceptability, prevalence rates, and performance in the MECA study. *Journal of the American Academy of Child and Adolescent Psychiatry* 35(7):865–867, 1996.
6. Kovacs, M., et al. Depressive disorders in childhood. I. A longitudinal prospective study of characteristics and recovery. *Archives of General Psychiatry* 41(3):229–237, 1984.
7. Weissman, M. M., et al. Depressed adolescents grow up. *Journal of the American Medical Association* 281:1701–1713, 1999.
8. Depression in children and adolescents: A fact sheet for physicians. National Institutes of Health, publication no. 00-744, September 2000.

9. Weller, E. B., et al. Aggressive behavior in patients with attention deficit/hyperactivity disorder, conduct disorder, and pervasive developmental disorder. *Journal of Clinical Psychiatry* 60:5–11, 1999.

10. Faraone, S. V., and Beiderman, J. Genetics of attention deficit hyperactivity disorder. *Child and Adolescent Clinics of North America* 2:285–301, 1994.

11. Carlson, G. A., Jenson, P. S., Nottleman, E. D., eds. Special issues: Current issues in childhood bipolarity. *Journal of Affective Disorders* 51, 1998.

12. Anderson, C. A., and Dill, K. E. Video games and aggressive behavior in the laboratory and in life. *Journal of Personality and Social Psychology* 78:4, 772–790, 2000.

13. Wallerstein, J., Lewis, J. M., and Blakeslee, S. *The Unexpected Legacy of Divorce.* Hyperion, 2000.

14. Wallerstein, J., and Blakeslee, S. *Second Chances: Men, Women, and Children a Decade After Divorce.* Houghton Mifflin, 1989.

Recommended Resources

Chapter Five: When Anger Runs Deeper

A.D.D. WareHouse Catalog at 1-800-233-9273 or 954-792-8944, or by writing 300 Northwest 70th Avenue, Suite 102, Plantation, FL 33317

American Foundation for Suicide Prevention, *www.afsp.org*.

CHADD (Children & Adults with Attention Deficit/Hyperactivity Disorder). Contact them at 8181 Professional Place, Suite 201, Landover, MD 20785, or call 800-233-4050 or 301-306-7070. *www.chadd.org*.

David G. Fassler, M.D. and Lynne S. Dumas, *Help Me, I'm Sad* (Penguin Putnam), 1998.

Barbara D. Ingersoll, Ph.D. and Sam Goldstein, Ph.D., *Lonely, Sad and Angry: A Parent's Guide to Depression in Children and Adolescents* (Doubleday), 1996.

Harold S. Koplewicz, M.D., *It's Nobody's Fault: New Hope and Help for Difficult Children* (Times Books/Random House), 1997.

Larry B. Silver, M.D., *Dr. Larry Silver's Advice on ADHD* (Times Books/Random House), 1999.

Chapter Six: Media and Society Messages

American Academy of Pediatrics website, *www.aap.org.*

Joanne Cantor, Ph.D., *Mommy, I'm Scared: How TV and Movies Frighten Children and What We Can Do to Protect Them* (Harvest Books), 1998.

Center for Media Education website, *www.cme.org/cme.*

James T. Hamilton, *Channeling Violence: The Economic Market for Violent TV Programming* (Princeton University Press), 1998.

John Leonard, *Smoke & Mirrors: Violence, Television & Other American Cultures* (New Press), 1998.

Madeline Levine, *See No Evil: A Guide to Protecting Our Children from Media Violence* (Jossey-Bass), 1998.

TV Parental Guidelines, *www.tvguidelines.org.*

Resources for Children

Aliki, *Feelings* (Greenwillow), 1986.

Jan and Stan Berenstain, *The Berenstain Bears and Too Much TV* (Random House), 1984.

Pat Thomas, *Stop Picking on Me—A First Look at Bullying* (Barron's), 2000.

Periodical Resources

Brad J. Bushman, Roy F. Baumeister, and Angela D. Stack, "Catharsis, aggression, and persuasive influence: Self-fulfilling or self-defeating prophecies?" *Journal of Personality and Social Psychology,* 76:(3):367–76, January 1999.

Daniel Okrent, "Raising Kids Online: What Can Parents Do?" *Time,* May 10, 1999, 38–59.

Chapter Ten: Divorce Wars

Marc J. Ackerman, Ph.D., *"Does Wednesday Mean Mom's House or Dad's?"* (Wiley), 1996.

Craig Everett and Sandra Volgy Everett, *Healthy Divorce* (Jossey-Bass), 1998.

Mel Krantzler, Ph.D., and Pat Krantzler, M.A., *The New Creative Divorce* (Adams), 1998.

Vicky Lansky, *Vicky Lansky's Divorce Book for Parents: Helping Your Child Cope with Divorce and Its Aftermath* (Book Peddlers), 1996.

M. Gary Neuman with Patricia Romanowski, *Helping Your Kids Cope with Divorce the Sandcastles Way* (Times Books/Random House), 1999.

Loriann Hoff Oberlin, *Surviving Separation and Divorce: A Woman's Guide to Making It Through the First Year* (Adams), 2000.

Isolina Ricci, Ph.D., *Mom's House, Dad's House* (Fireside), 1997.

Diana Shulman, *Co-parenting After Divorce: How to Raise Happy, Healthy Children in Two-Home Families* (Winspeed Press), 1997.

Judith S. Wallerstein and Sandra Blakeslee, *Second Chances: Men, Women and Children a Decade After Divorce* (Houghton Mifflin), 1996.

Judith Wallerstein, Julia M. Lewis, and Sandra Blakeslee, *The Unexpected Legacy of Divorce* (Hyperion), 2000.

Resources for Children

Vicky Lansky, *It's Not Your Fault, Koko Bear: A Read-Together Book for Parents & Young Children During Divorce* (Book Peddlars), 1998.

Fred M. Rogers, *Let's Talk About It: Divorce* (Family Communications), 1998.

———. *Let's Talk About It: Stepfamilies* (Family Communications), 1997.

"Talking with Families About Divorce," a free brochure. Send a business-size, self-addressed, stamped envelope to Family Communications, Inc., 4802 Fifth Avenue, Pittsburgh, PA 15213 or call 412-687-2990.

Index

Violent crimes, 106
Visitation, 219, 225–226, 229

Wallerstein, Judith S., 219, 222
Walsh, David, 136
Wellbutrin, 121
What's Heaven? (Shriver), 83

Whining, 201–202
    tactic in arguments, 165–166
Winning, as goal of argument, 150–152
Wolfelt, Alan D., 83

You're imagining things tactic in
    arguments, 164–165

About the Authors

DR. TIM MURPHY is a father, husband, one of eleven children, psychologist, and state senator. As a psychologist, he has a private practice and has been affiliated with Children's Hospital of Pittsburgh, Mercy Hospital, and has served as assistant professor of pediatrics at the University of Pittsburgh School of Medicine. He is currently on the adjunct faculty of the University of Pittsburgh. As a state senator, he is chairman of the Aging and Youth Committee, is vice chairman of the Committee on Public Health and Welfare, and has focused many of his legislative efforts on issues affecting children and families. He is the only senator in the country who is a practicing psychologist. He has appeared on hundreds of television and radio programs and written numerous articles on family concerns. Dr. Murphy lives in suburban Pittsburgh with his wife, Nan, and their daughter, Bevin.

LORIANN HOFF OBERLIN is the author of *Writing for Money; Working at Home While the Kids Are There, Too; The Insider's Guide to Pittsburgh;* and *Surviving Separation and Divorce: A Woman's Guide to Making It Through the First Year.* She has written a monthly column on work and family for the *Pittsburgh Business Times* and contributes to national magazines on a variety of subjects. Ms. Oberlin has two sons.